BERNIE BOSTON

BERNIE BOSTON
AMERICAN PHOTOJOURNALIST

THERESE MULLIGAN

RIT CARY GRAPHIC ARTS PRESS
ROCHESTER, NY

Bernie Boston: American Photojournalist
Therese Mulligan

Copyright © 2006 Rochester Institute of Technology,
Cary Graphic Arts Press, and individual authors. All rights reserved.

No part of this book may be reproduced in any manner without written
permission of the publisher, except in the case of brief quotations.

Published and distributed by
RIT Cary Graphic Arts Press
90 Lomb Memorial Drive
Rochester, New York 14623-5604
http://library.rit.edu/cary/carypress.html

Every reasonable effort has been made to contact
copyright holders of materials reproduced in this book.
Corrections should be addressed to RIT Cary Graphic Arts Press.

Front cover: Photograph by Bernie Boston.
Back cover: Portrait of Bernie Boston by Ken Heinen.

Printed in the United States by Rochester Offset Press
ISBN-10 1-933360-19-4
ISBN-13 978-1-933360-19-5

Library of Congress Cataloging-in-Publication Data

Mulligan, Therese.
    Bernie Boston : American photojournalist / Therese Mulligan.
       p. cm.
    ISBN-13: 978-1-933360-19-5 (pbk.)
    ISBN-10: 1-933360-19-4 (pbk.)
    1. Photojournalism–United States–Exhibitions. 2. Boston, Bernie,
  1933—Exhibitions. I. Title.
  TR820.M86 2006
  779.092–dc22
                                        2006027021

CONTENTS

FOREWORD

Bernie Boston is a gentleman, in the most regal sense. He can walk into a room without many heads turning. But, given a few minutes of genuine hand-shaking and polite introductions, people begin to listen. A soft voice seemingly whispers as he opens conversations. That is when one realizes that this man is genuinely interested in getting to know those around him.

His camera draped over his shoulder is so comfortable it has become part of his wardrobe. I have not seen him without it even in many late-evening, darkened dining rooms, while enjoying conversation over dessert. He is still making photographs every day. He feels compelled to shoot daily because he is a photojournalist. As Bernie says, "Hey, that is what we do, every day."

A down-to-earth photographer who is interested in what is going on around him, as well as across the country, Bernie has been able to be in the right spot for much of his life. Or, is it that he realizes that his selection of location is one of the most critical aspects of his storytelling? As you review his life's history of imagery, I think you will see the wisdom that he has shown in choosing the right spot most of the time.

Discussing the role of a photographer with Bernie is just the beginning of his story. As a former White House news photographer, he can elucidate on special moments in his career that became spellbinding stories. These stories are never political statements or politically-charged comments. This gentleman can bring out the emotion and personal observation of the moment without stepping on or over the line. Did that come from working in those highly-charged, tumultuous years known as the 1960s? After listening to his stories, you feel that it really came from growing up within a sensitive, caring family.

While Bernie Boston tells stories with his camera, he is also willing to tell the stories of how photographers can become successful and make a difference. This book of images is an opportunity for all of us to understand and celebrate Bernie's story, but it is really only the beginning of another story.

I am proud to share the news that, while this book and exhibition of his work represent Bernie's life with the camera, a deeper story is unfolding. Bernie has presented his total photographic archive to RIT. That includes the images you see here and others that will also be housed in a special Bernie Boston collection at the university's Wallace Library.

RIT students will have the opportunity to study this imagery in detail. What image was captured just before *Flower Power*? What image followed on the same roll of film? Through thoughtful study, they will be able to see how the photographer's mind took in all that was happening and captured different images to represent the scene, and then reevaluate the images that made it through the editing process. That opportunity will be an exceptional learning experience.

Thus Bernie Boston allows us to review his creative and thinking processes. As a picture-maker and a storyteller he has proven powerful. As we take a look at all of these images we will see the true power behind that camera. Thank you, Bernie, for all that you continue to do for RIT.

William W. DuBois
Administrative Chair, Photographic Arts
School of Photographic Arts and Sciences
Rochester Institute of Technology

ACKNOWLEDGMENTS

Every publication is the result of the dedication, talent and energy of an ensemble of individuals. I wish to thank the School of Photographic Arts and Sciences (SPAS) at Rochester Institute of Technology (RIT), and especially its Chair, Bill DuBois, for his support throughout every phase of the production of this publication and accompanying exhibition. My deep appreciation goes to Becky Simmons, RIT Archivist, for her professional assistance and friendship, and Nick Savot, student assistant, for his archival skills.

A special acknowledgment to RIT Cary Graphic Arts Press and its staff: David Pankow, Director; Amelia Hugill-Fontanel, Production Editor; and Marnie Soom, Design and Marketing Specialist. I greatly appreciate their invaluable assistance and collegial spirit throughout the book's production. Thanks to Elizabeth Lamark, Visual Resources Manager, for her expertise in the creation of the reproductions for this publication. I am especially grateful to Patricia Cost and Carla Williams, who skillfully edited the book's content. The support of RIT's Development Department enabled this book, and its accompanying exhibition, to become a reality. I extend my appreciation to Heather Engel, Assistant Vice President for Principal and Planned Giving and Peter Gabak, Development Officer, College of Imaging Arts and Sciences.

Students in the MFA Program in Imaging Arts greatly contributed their enthusiasm and skills to the organization and installation of the exhibition. I wish to thank John Aäsp, Jayson Bimber, and the SPAS Gallery staff.

The *Los Angeles Times* granted permission for the reproduction of published news photographs by Boston. I am grateful for their support of this publication. Nikon Professional Services generously contributed to this publication's realization. Its support is an example of a continued dedication to photography, in both the professional and educational realm.

Finally, I am greatly indebted to Bernie Boston and his wife, Peggy. I deeply appreciate their trust with organizing their archive for presentation in this publication. For their abiding support and friendship, I am truly grateful.

Bernie Boston extends his heartfelt gratitude to wife, Peggy, and his parents, Lewis (Dick) R. Boston and Norrine W. Boston. He also thanks the instructors and professors in the School of Photographic Arts and Sciences who guided his photographic studies and supported his life's dedication to the field of photojournalism.

THE ESSENCE OF PICTURING HISTORY

THE PHOTOJOURNALISM OF BERNIE BOSTON

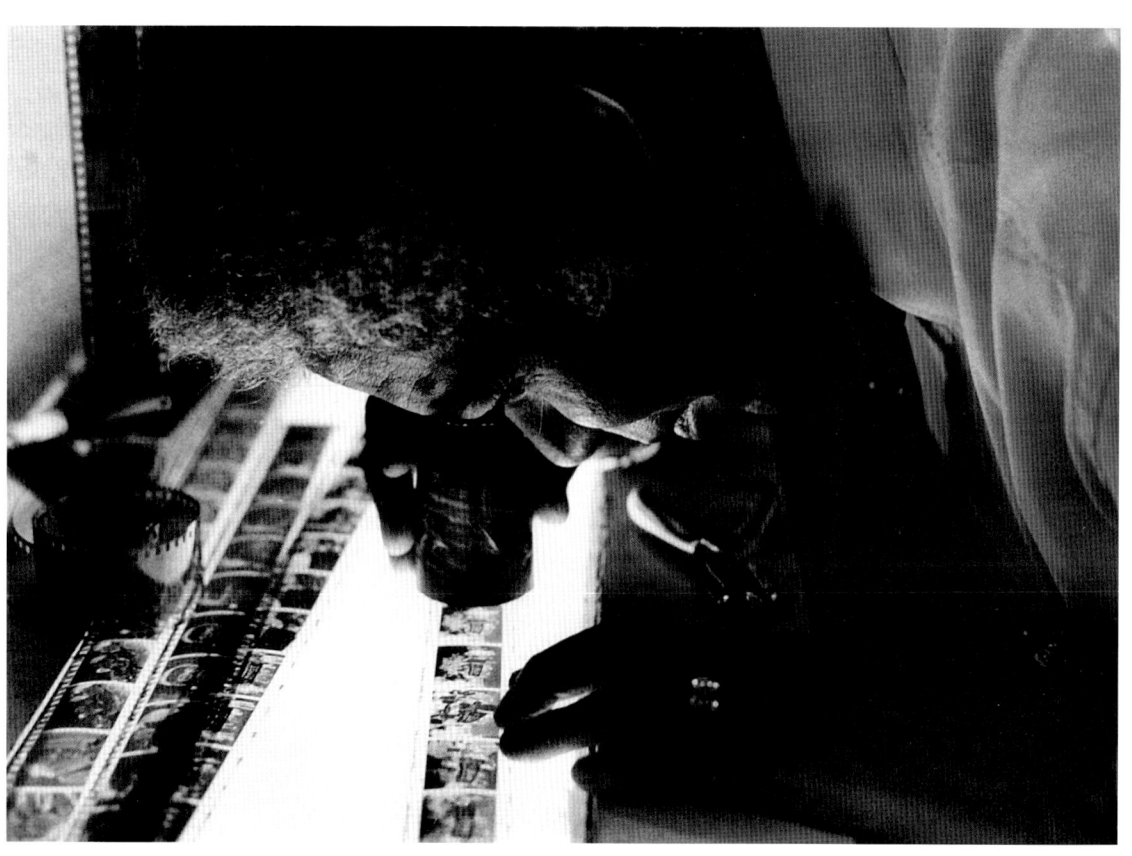

For the photojournalist, capturing a culturally charged event is analogous to the fortuitous alignment of celestial bodies—or so it might seem to viewers. However, in a photojournalist's repertoire, luck is less a consequential player than a trained instinct for arresting a heightened moment drawn from unfolding human experience: an instinct that bores into the very essence of a specific time and place. The photojournalistic notion of capturing the "essence" of an event was defined by one of the genre's greatest practitioners, Henri Cartier-Bresson, in his 1952 book *Images à la sauvette*. Best known by the English translation of its title for an American edition, *The Decisive Moment* influenced both the appearance and popularity of photography and photojournalism in the second half of the twentieth century. "To me," Cartier-Bresson wrote, "photography is the simultaneous recognition in a fraction of a second, of the significance of an event as well as of a precise organization of forms which give that event its proper expression." The substantial intertwining of time, fact and form, acute observation, and cultural expression was for Cartier-Bresson and successive generations of photojournalists the essence or *meaning* of a successfully rendered news photograph.

In the 1950s, the critical impact of *The Decisive Moment* coincided with an upswing in photographers pursuing careers in photojournalism. Hard-won recognition by practitioners employed by newspapers and popular picture magazines like *LIFE* had helped to define the genre's role as both a specialized discipline and a legitimate form of mass communication. As a consequence, American universities and colleges began to integrate photojournalism into their curriculums. One of the first to include it was Rochester Institute of Technology (RIT). In 1952, RIT's Department of Photographic Technology added pictorial journalism to its growing, career-based educational programs of advertising, technology, and science. Located in Rochester, NY, the university benefited from a close association with area industries such as Eastman Kodak Company, which had established

Bruce Sittle
Bernie Boston, chief photographer for the *Washington Star,* looking over negatives from an assignment at the community light table in the *Star* lab. July, 1981.

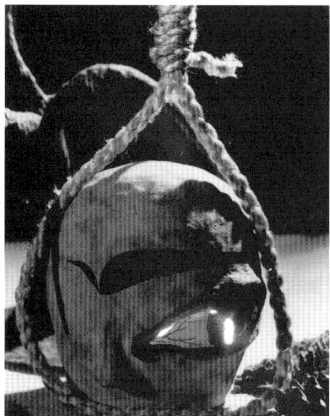

[Lighting assignment]
ca. 1950s

working relationships with photographers, including photojournalists. Such associations provided a significant enhancement to professional training with first-rate facilities, access to a multitude of equipment and materials, and photography specialists, including Eastman Kodak employees.

Due to its prescient acknowledgment of the evolving disciplines of photography, RIT became a mecca for photographers of every stripe, in particular fledgling photojournalists. One such photographer was Washington, DC, native Bernie Boston, whose fascination for photojournalism began as a teenager, when he participated in the Scholastic Sports Association, sponsored by the *Washington Daily News*.

Although he graduated in 1955 with a degree in photographic science, Boston developed his student reportage skills alongside RIT's emergent journalism curriculum. Beyond the rigors of the classroom, he chronicled school activities including dances, athletic events, and meetings of Delta Lambda Epsilon, the professional photography fraternity he co-founded. Journalistic experience and exposure gained during these formative years laid the professional groundwork for Boston's celebrated career as a photojournalist, formally begun in 1963 as a staff photographer for the *Dayton* (Ohio) *Daily News*.

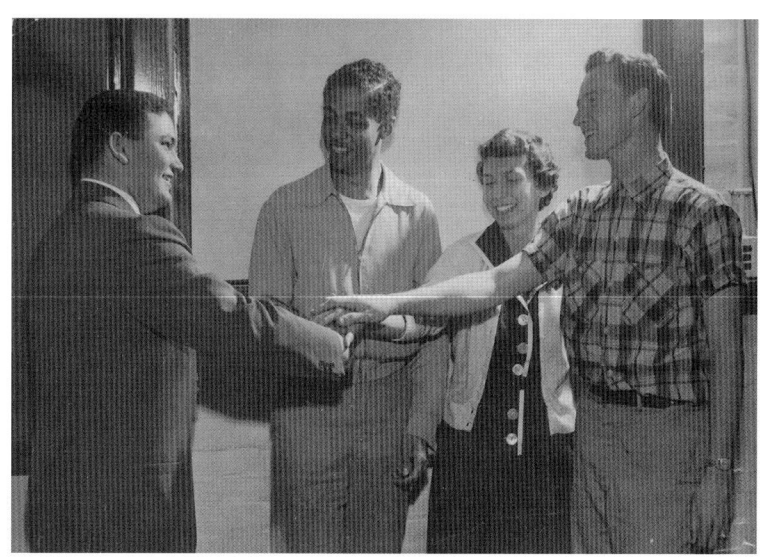

Unidentified photographer
[Bernie Boston and classmates at Rochester Institute of Technology.]
ca. 1950s

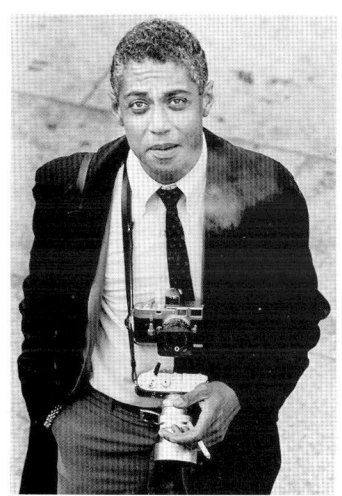

Ken Heinen
[Bernie Boston with cameras around
his neck and a cigarette in his left hand.]
1963

During the 1960s, American photojournalists did not have to look far for potent subjects that would prove to be of significant historic consequence. City streets and small-town squares exploded with demonstrations supporting the Civil Rights and anti-Vietnam War movements. Not since the Great Depression had the fabric of American society been so deeply torn by public dissention and strife. Print photojournalists like Boston, as well as the new media rival of broadcast journalism, aggressively covered the tumultuous American scene, prompting a new public awareness of the power of the picture press and broadcast news to shape popular opinion.

In 1967, the year he took up a new position as staff photographer for Washington, DC-based the *Washington Star* (also known as the *Washington Star-News* and the *Evening Star*), Boston was immersed in covering the personalities and events shaping the Civil Rights movement. His 1967 portrait of Black Panther Justice Minister H. Rap Brown is a pictorial testament to the activist's combative nature. Brown was famous for a fiery rhetoric, including the declaration, "If America don't come around, we're gonna burn it down."   This seemingly clandestine portrait of the self-assured activist stands in contrast to Boston's candidly ardent portrait of another civil rights leader, Martin Luther King, Jr., captured while speaking to Poor People's Campaign supporters in the months preceding his assassination on April 4, 1968. The nation's capitol was the culminating site for many public protests including the Poor People's Campaign, a cross-country demonstration organized by King and the Southern Christian Leadership Conference to address social and economic inequality.

A multitude of memorable images give voice to this important moment in American history, including portraits of pioneering activists Coretta Scott King, Jesse Jackson, and Hosea Williams, views of Poor People's Campaign marchers, the Campaign's mule train, and the enclave of Resurrection City, a tent town raised by Campaign participants within site of the Washington Monument. As a coda to the unfinished work initiated by the Civil Rights movement, Boston produced *Poverty in Washington, DC Project*, a deeply affecting photographic essay chronicling the capital's troubled neighborhoods and a disenfranchised African American populace.

At the *Star*, Boston's beat included documenting public fervor over the United States' growing involvement in East Asia. At a 1967 demonstration outside the Pentagon, he seized upon a dramatic scene of a standoff

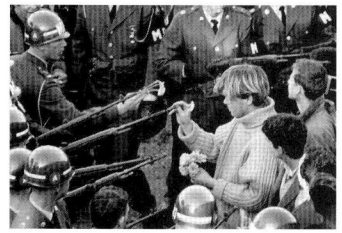

Flower Power
1967

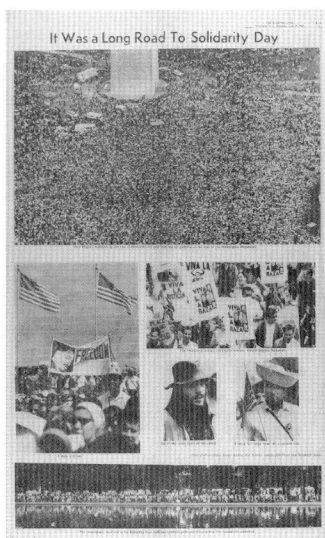

[Poor People's March]
Full-page layout, the *Evening Star*,
Washington, DC, June 19, 1968.

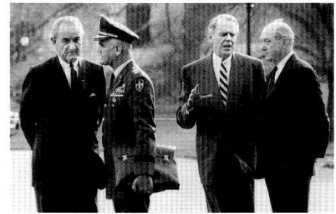

[President Johnson and staff]
1968

between a rifle-bearing National Guard detail and youthful activists with flowers. Better known as *Flower Power*, this is Boston's most recognized photograph. A second-place award winner for the Pulitzer Prize—photojournalism's most august accolade—the anti-Vietnam War image is emblematic of a "decisive moment," the photojournalistic paradigm of time and form meaningfully combined with vital cultural expression. Boston recorded the tense scene at the precise moment demonstrators placed blooms in the soldiers' rifle barrels. With its publication, *Flower Power* gained the status of cultural icon, a resonating touchstone of young Americans' newfound influence in determining political and social discourse.

The stunning press coverage of national events in the 1960s secured numerous photojournalistic careers, including those of Boston, Flip Schulke, Charles Moore, and Bruce Davidson, another RIT graduate. For many, powerful news agencies such as the Associated Press, Reuters, or Magnum (a photojournalist-led consortium) were the primary outlet for dissemination of news photography to international media. For others like Boston, contracting to a major newspaper offered a continuity of career with opportunities of unique professional advancement: the *Washington Star* was Boston's home base until 1981. In 1971, he was named its director of photography, heading a staff of photographers. Significantly, his prodigious work gained him access to the rarified realm of Washington, DC's most famous residence—the White House—and the prized credentials of White House news photographer.

The highly complex, emotionally charged national stage of Washington politics poses unusual challenges for a White House news photographer. A keen understanding of personalities and events, and a descriptive vision for a telling gesture, pose and situation, enable a photojournalist to capture the heart of a story, so that it becomes easily understandable to the widest number of people. Boston's 1968 view of President Lyndon Johnson with Chief of Staff General William Westmoreland, Secretary of Defense Clifford Clark (who had recently replaced Robert McNamara), and Secretary of State Dean Rusk reveals a tattered administration buffeted by the escalating Vietnam conflict. Within months of this picture, Johnson, on March 31, 1968, televised his decision not to run for a second term as president.

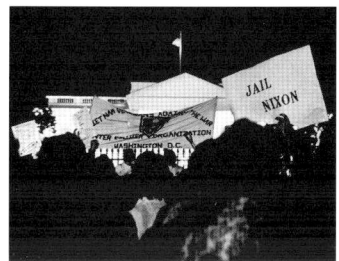

[Nixon resigns]
1974

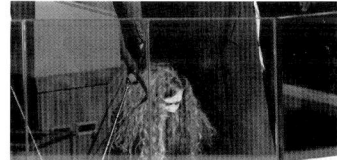
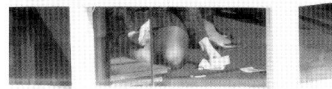

[Chelsea Clinton]
1993

The televised announcement of another president, Richard Nixon, prompted Boston to capture a very different ensemble photograph on August 9, 1974. On the night of Nixon's resignation speech, Boston situated himself in front of the White House. Between his camera and the blazing lights of the President's residence, demonstrators, holding placards inscribed with words silently shouting for Nixon's resignation, gathered to protest the abuse of power of the President and his administration. In gesture, time and place, Boston's shadowy photograph is a compelling portrait of the anger of the American people on one of the darkest days in the nation's history.

Photographs of presidents fill Boston's archive. Over four decades, as a White House news photographer for the *Washington Star*, and, beginning in 1981, as the Washington bureau photographer for the *Los Angeles Times*, he photographed seated presidents from Lyndon Johnson to Bill Clinton. A primary aim of his work was to distill and portray the intimate character of each president, not the well-honed persona specially designed for media consumption. Boston's ability to extract the essence of his subject is hauntingly apparent in his portrait of President Jimmy Carter in an unguarded moment of inner contemplation, in President Reagan's surprising and angry outburst during a news conference, and in Reagan and his wife's frank emotional response during a memorial service held for U.S. marines killed in an attack on their barracks in Lebanon in 1983.

Time and again, Boston discovered new pictorial ways to relate familiar stories. One such example is the playful relationship of two photographs from President Bill Clinton's inaugural ceremony. In one image, Clinton is caught delivering his speech in mid-sentence, illuminating the power of his oratory. In the other, Clinton's young daughter, Chelsea, crouches in a sentimental gesture to pick up her father's speech notes fallen from the lectern. Together, these two images elucidate the public and private importance of the event for a newly elected President and his family.

In addition to portraits, Boston chronicled the momentous activities shaping a president's tenure in office. In several photographs, he documented the shocking events surrounding the assassination attempt on President Reagan's life on March 30, 1981, and the gunshot injuries suffered by James Brady, Reagan's assistant and press secretary. A complementary set of images record the two men's recuperation and the celebratory

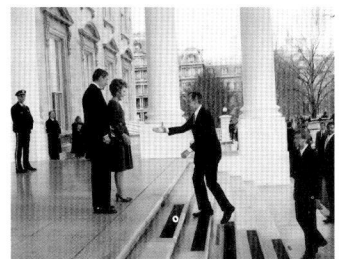

[Reagan and Bush]
1989

welcomes received at the end of their respective hospitalizations. Political scandals involving presidential administrations were also part of Boston's assignment, including the 1987 Congressional hearings on the Iran-Contra Affair and the testimony of its most public figure, Lt. Col. Oliver North. In addition, Boston surveyed state events: the signing of the Middle East Peace Accord with President Clinton, Israel's Yitzhak Rabin and the Palestine Liberation Organization's Yassar Arafat; and Reagan's conveyance of the Presidential residence to President-elect George Bush and Vice President-elect Dan Quayle.

Photographic reportage is synonymous with picturing history. For Boston, picturing history was not merely measured in portraits of presidents, activists, and newsmakers including Supreme Court Justice Sandra Day O'Connor, Pope John Paul II, and photographer/filmmaker Gordon Parks. It also consisted of events of dazzling human endeavor, such as the returning flight of Columbia, the first American space shuttle, or quiet moments of human remembrance, like the mournful visit of a mother to the Vietnam Memorial or the prayer of a Kennedy family nanny standing at the graveside of Robert F. Kennedy. Throughout his career, Boston has demonstrated that the essence of picturing history is to seize upon its most telling and crucial human element, whether the event or personality is spectacular or commonplace. He continues this approach today as photographer and publisher with his wife, Peggy, who serves as editor, of the *Bryce Mountain Courier*, a regional Virginia newspaper, and as one of America's most consummate photojournalists.

Therese Mulligan, Ph.D.
Director, School of Photographic Arts and Sciences Gallery
Rochester Institute of Technology

ENDNOTES
1   Fulton, Marianne. *Eyes of Time: Photojournalism in America*. New York: Little, Brown and Company, 1988.
2   H. Rap Brown, http://en.wikipedia.org/wiki/H._Rap_Brown, June 2006.

GALLERY

All works are by Bernie Boston (American, b. 1933, Washington, DC)
and appear courtesy of Bernie and Peggy Boston, unless otherwise noted.
All photographs are modern gelatin silver prints, with exceptions noted.

Each image in this publication is accompanied by a caption that indicates
published title and date. Often photographs here were given no title or date.
In such cases, a descriptive title is presented in brackets and, when known,
appropriate dates are included.

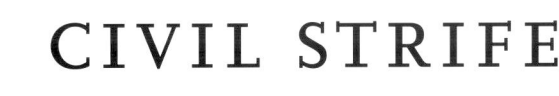

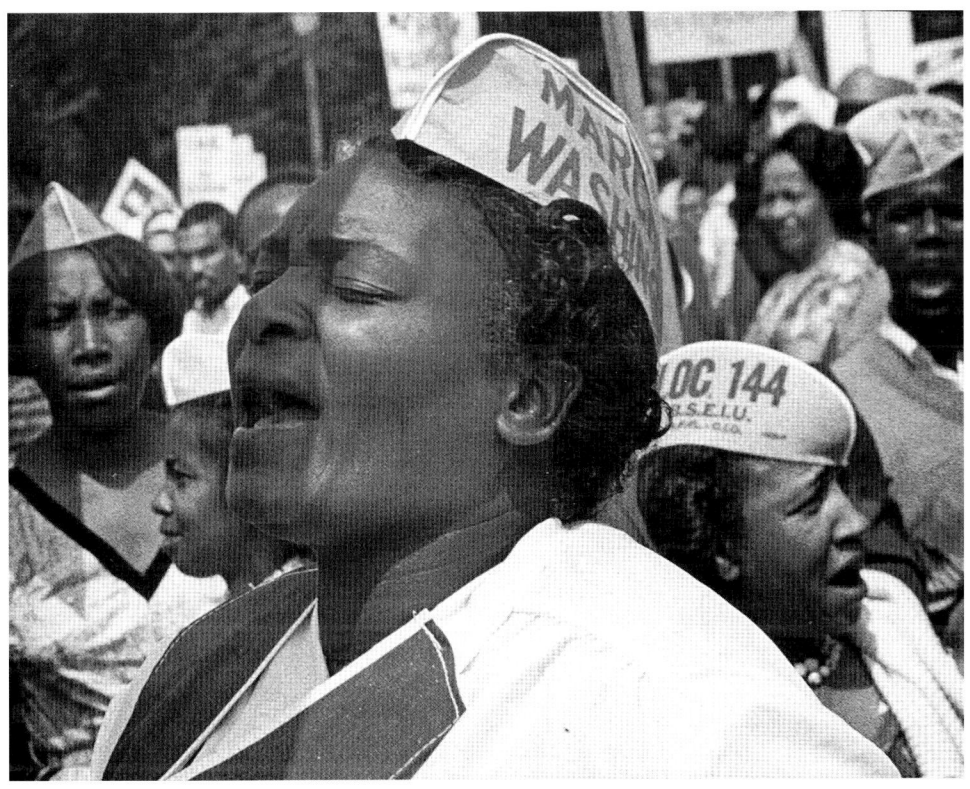

[Woman with "March on Washington"
Union hat.]
1963

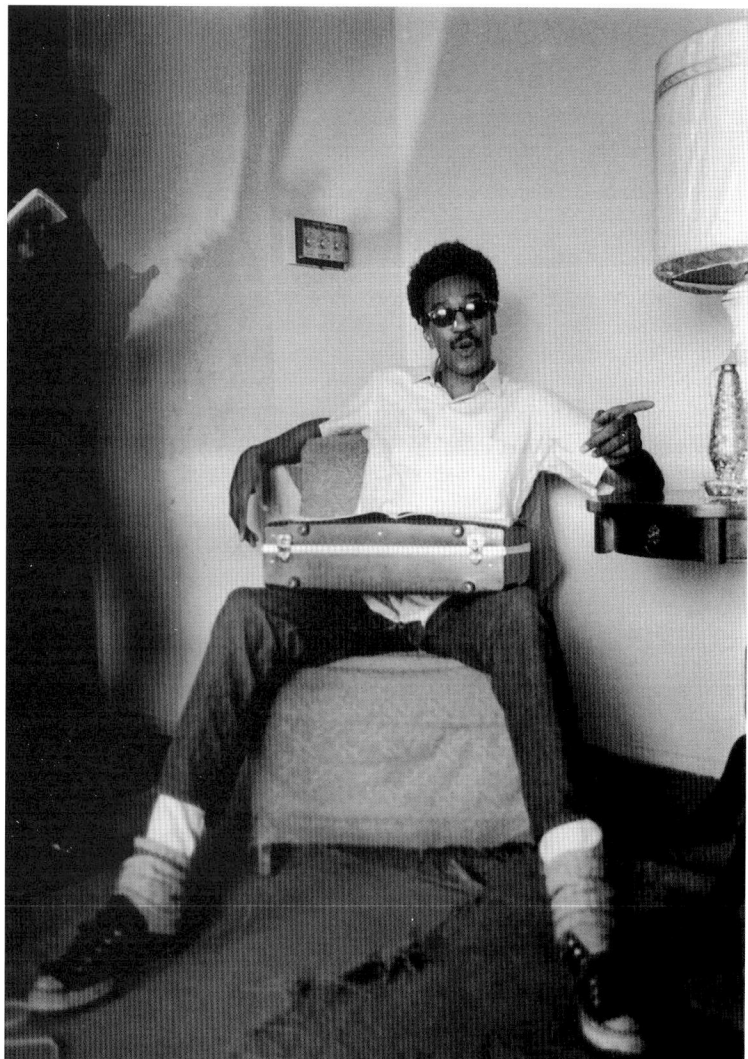

[Portrait of Black Panther leader
H. Rap Brown, June 15, 1967,
Dayton Daily News, Dayton, OH.]
1967

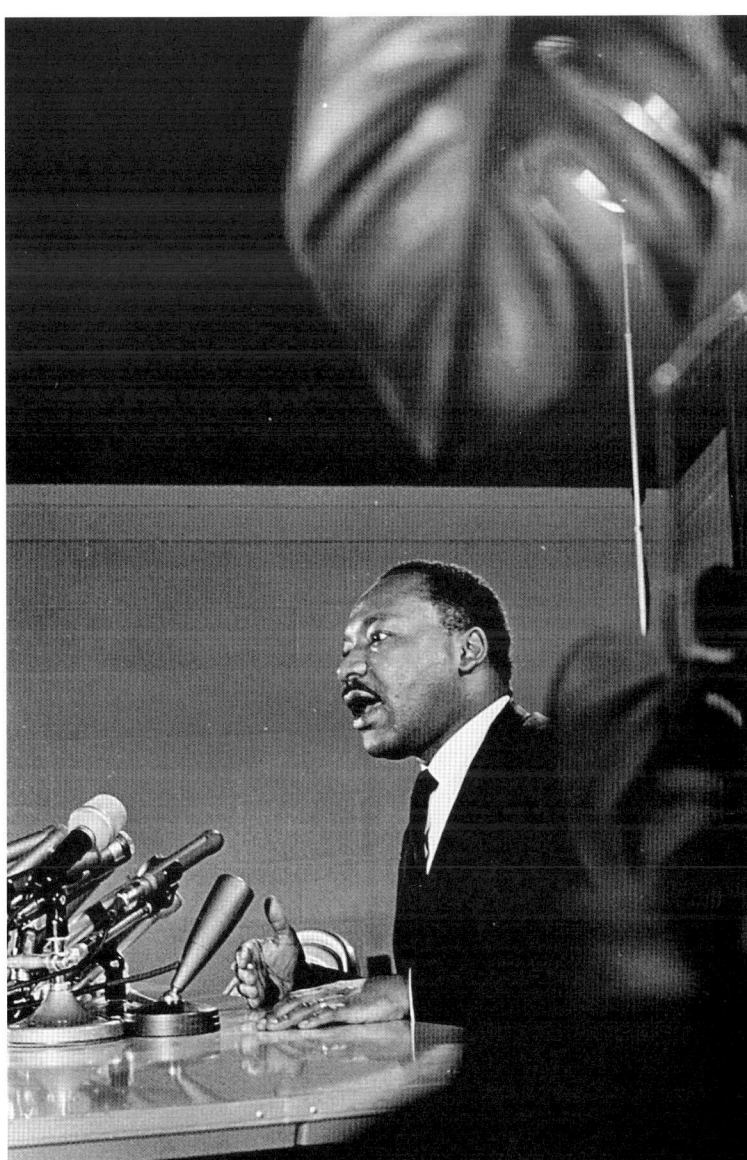

[Martin Luther King]
ca. 1960
Digital print

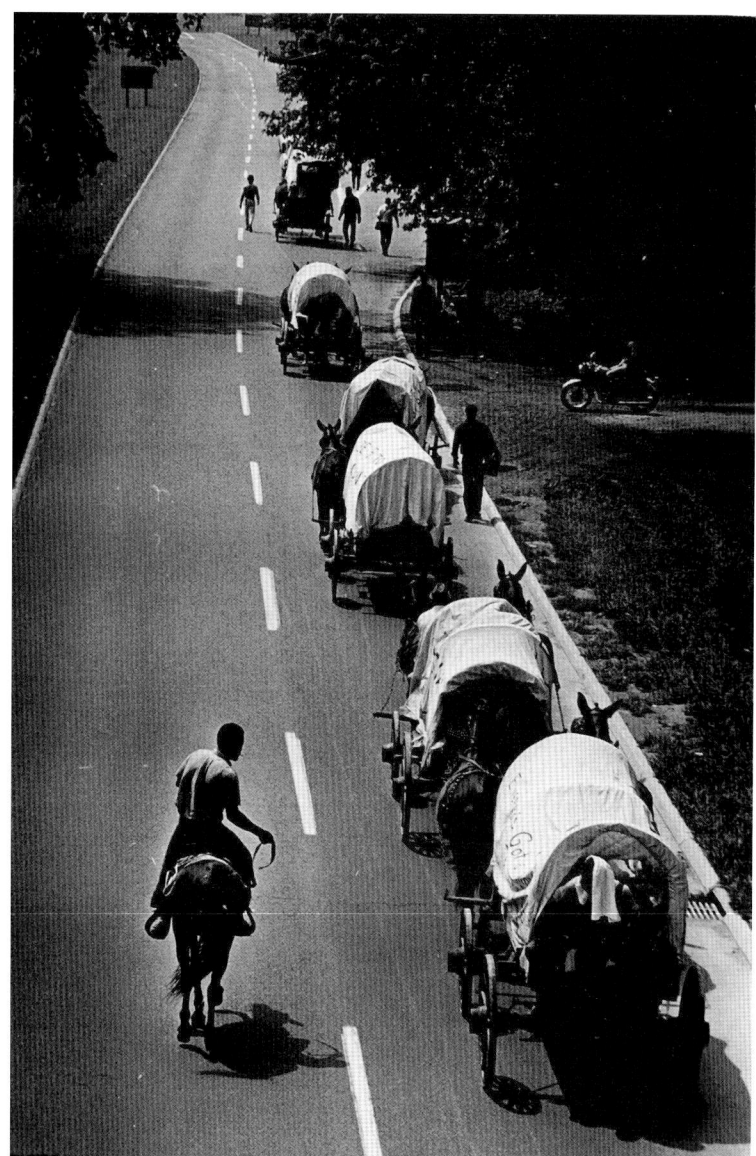

[Mule train, Poor People's Campaign.]
1968

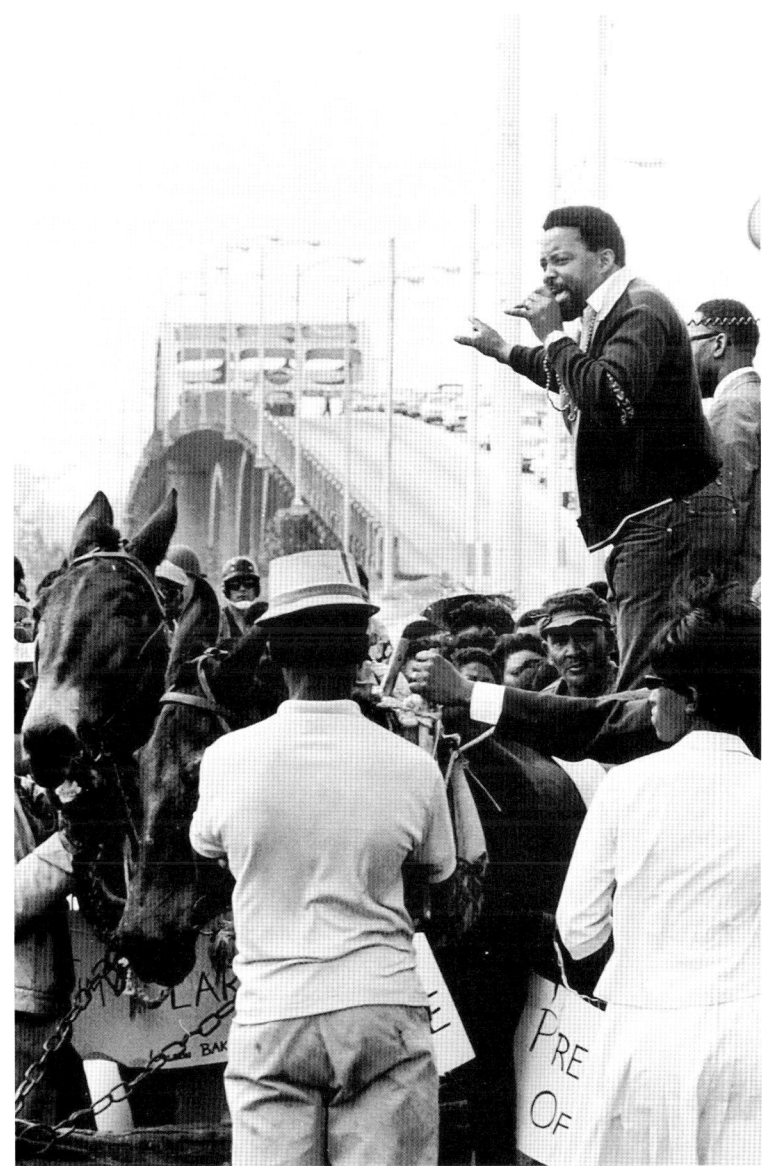

[Demonstrators, Edmund
Pettis Bridge, Selma, AL,
Poor People's Campaign.]
1968

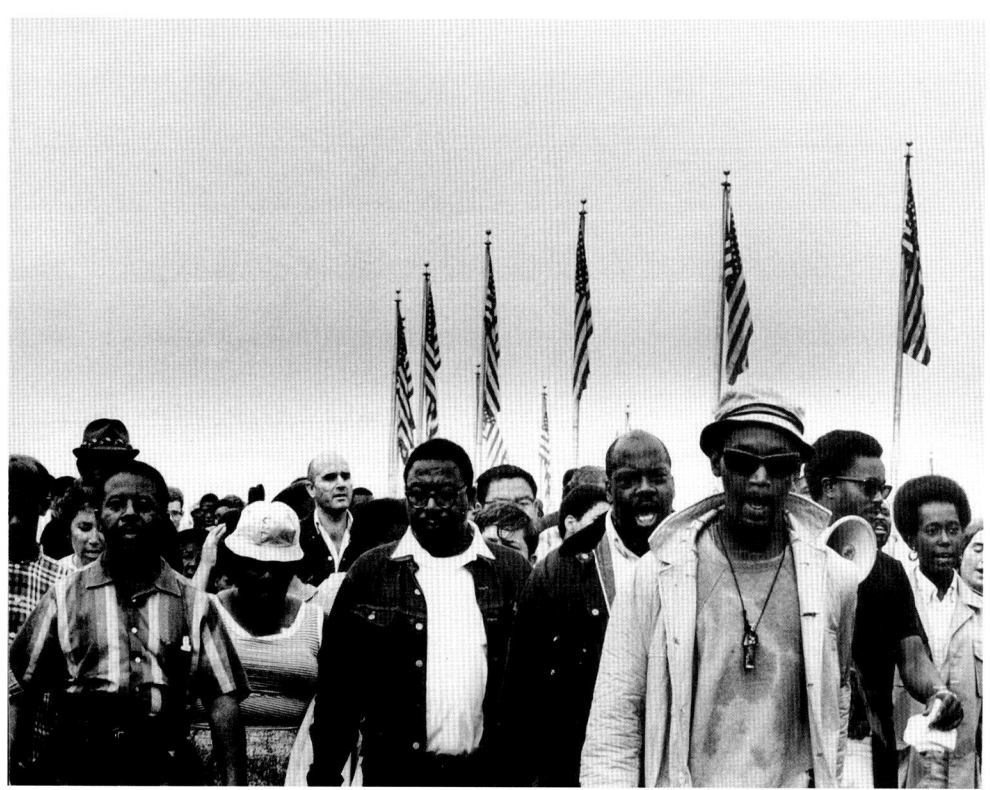

[March across Edmund Pettis Bridge,
Selma, AL. On the left is Hosea
Williams of the Southern Christian
Leadership Conference (SCLC).]
1968

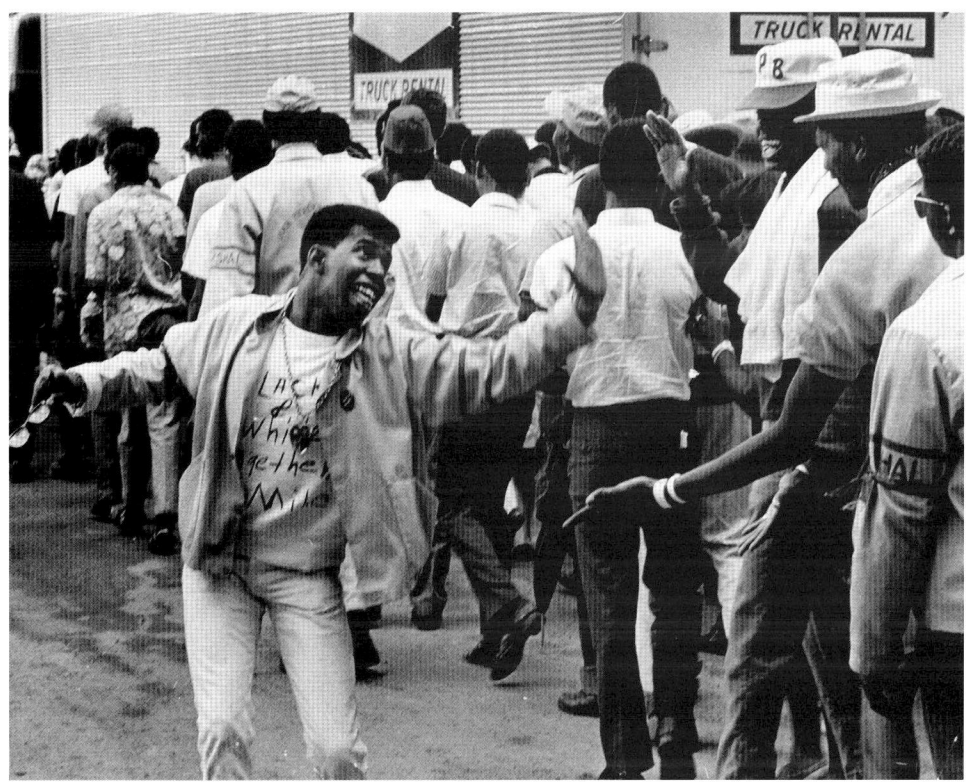

[Man on the street greeting
marchers at the Poor People's
Campaign, Washington, DC.]
1968

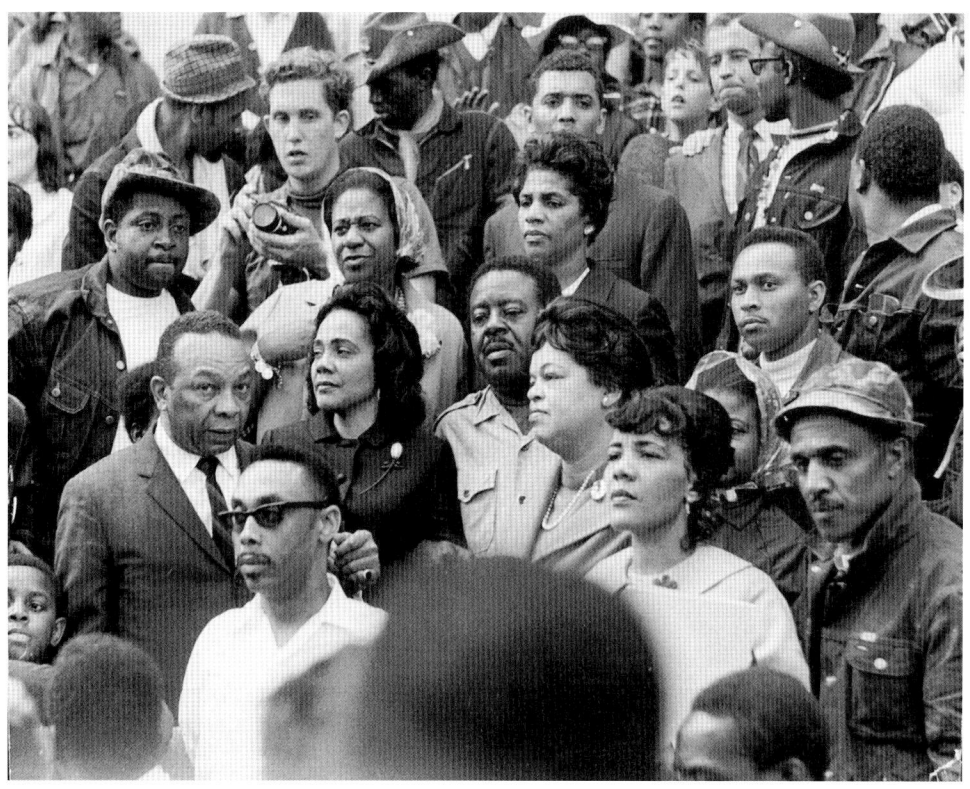

[Coretta Scott King with supporters,
(right, Hosea Williams, SCLC; left,
Walter Washington, Mayor of
Washington, DC) at the Poor People's
Campaign, Washington, DC.]
1968

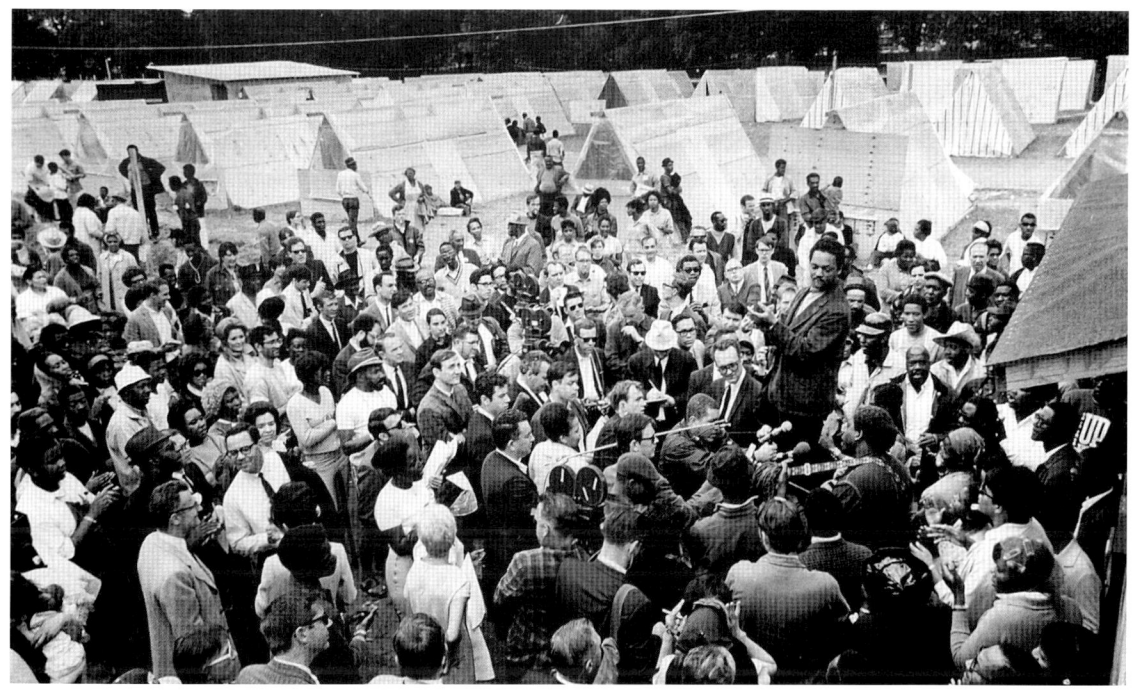

[Jesse Jackson and supporters meet
with the press at Resurrection City
during the Poor People's Campaign,
Washington, DC.]
1968

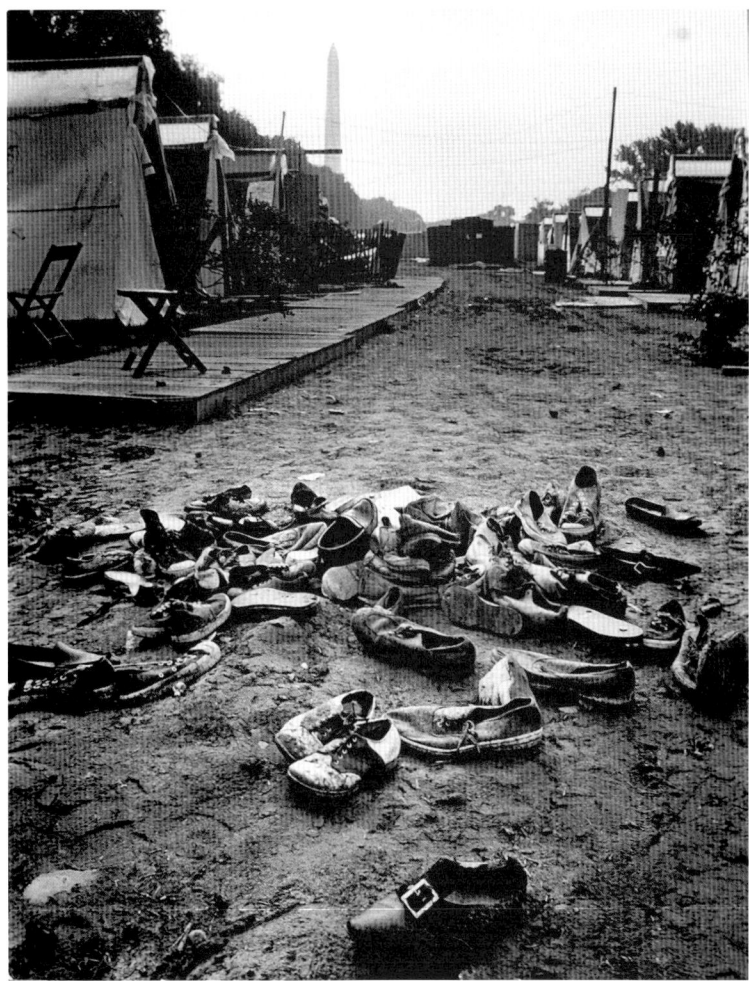

[Shoes, Resurrection City,
Poor People's Campaign,
Washington, DC.]
1968

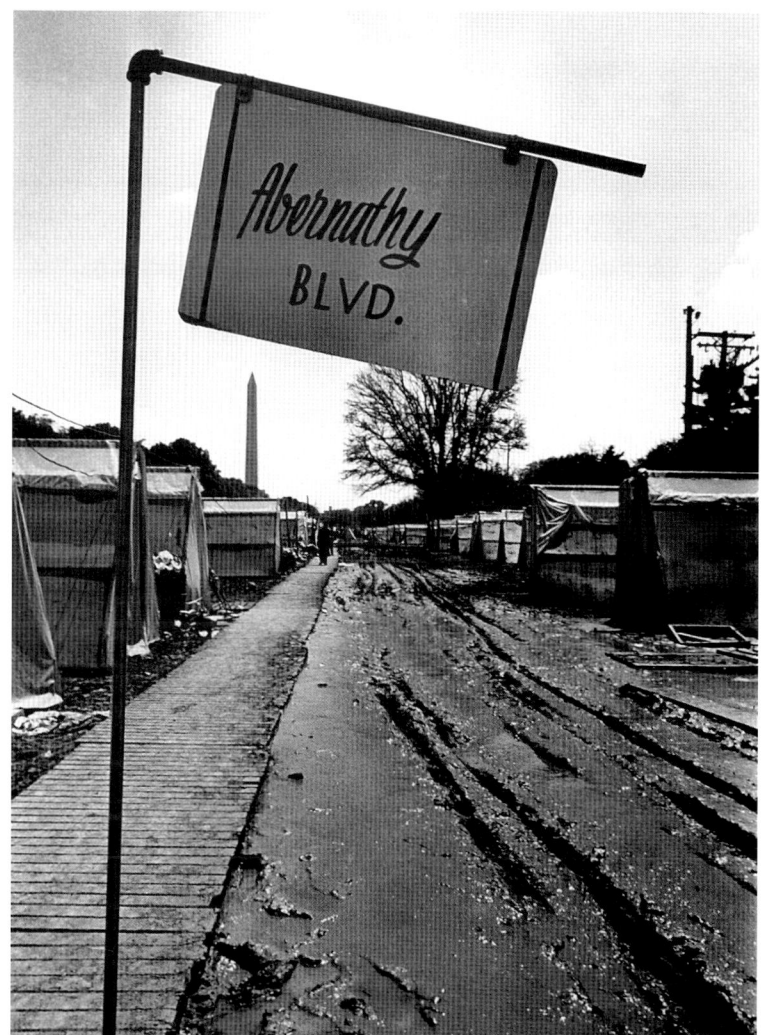

[Ralph Abernathy street sign in
Resurrection City, Poor People's
Campaign, Washington, DC.]
1968

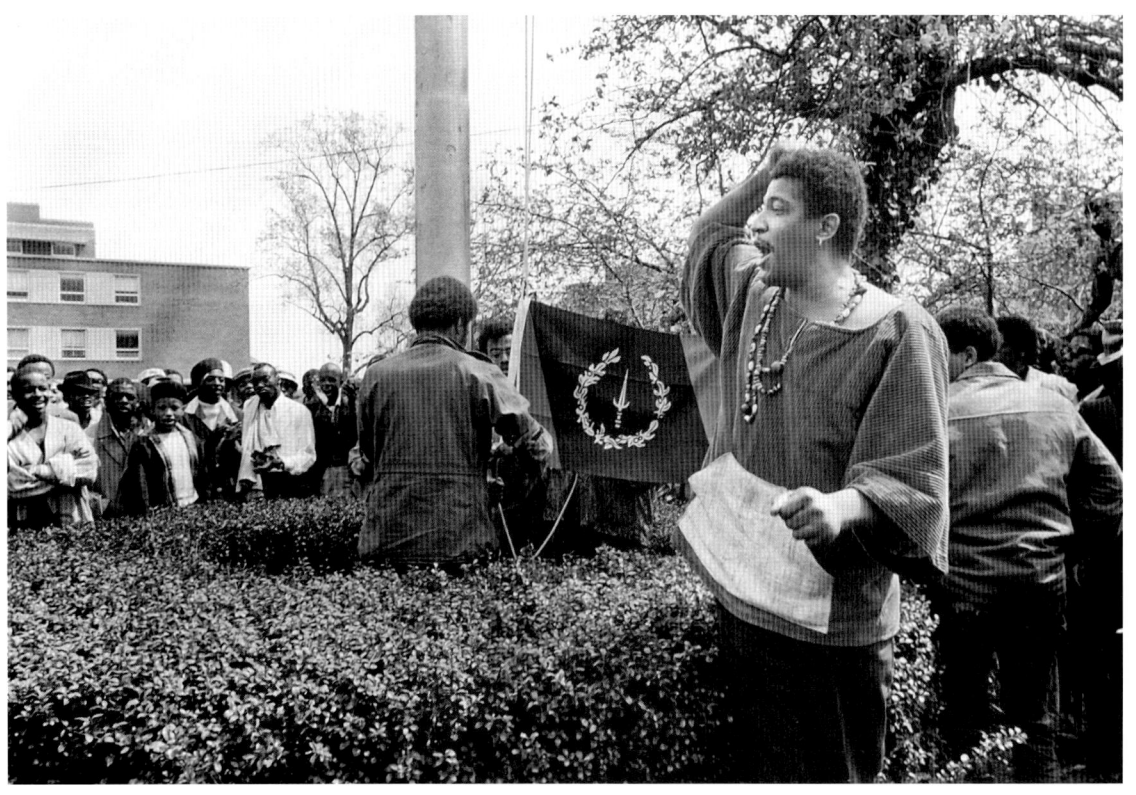

[Black Nationalists put up organization
flag after taking down U.S. flag at
Howard University at the beginning
of the April riots.]
1968

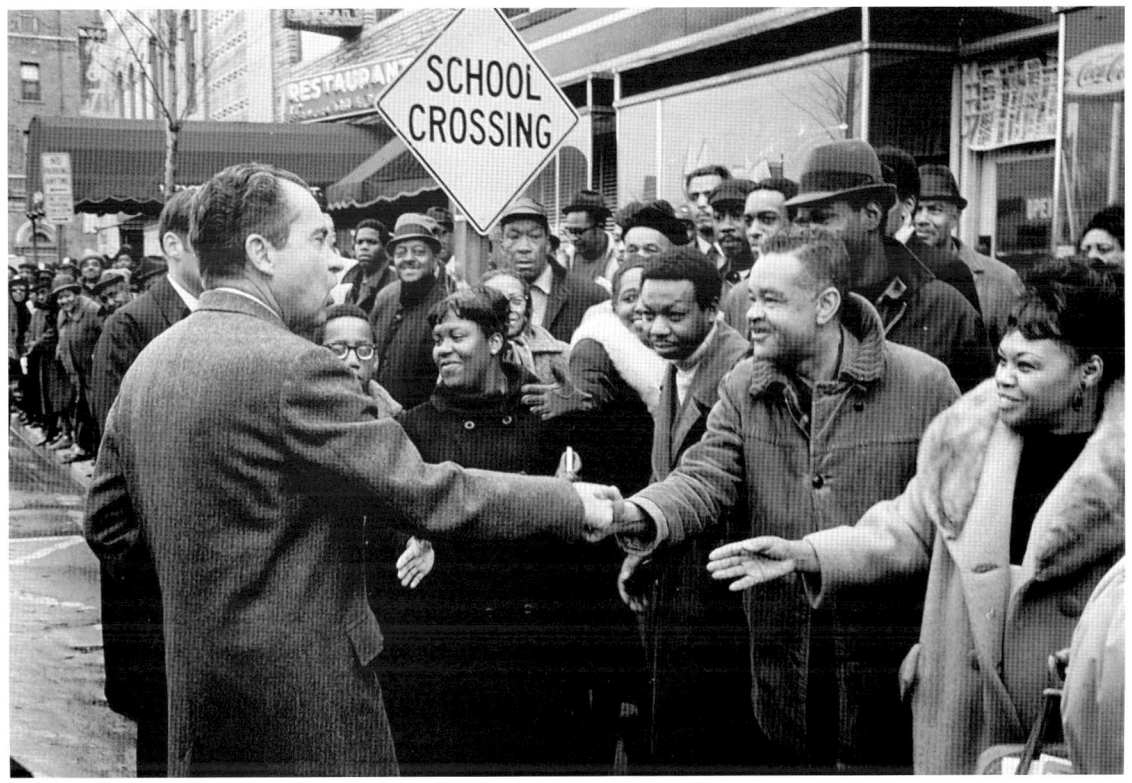

[Richard Nixon visits 7th Street in
Washington, DC, after the April riots.]
1968

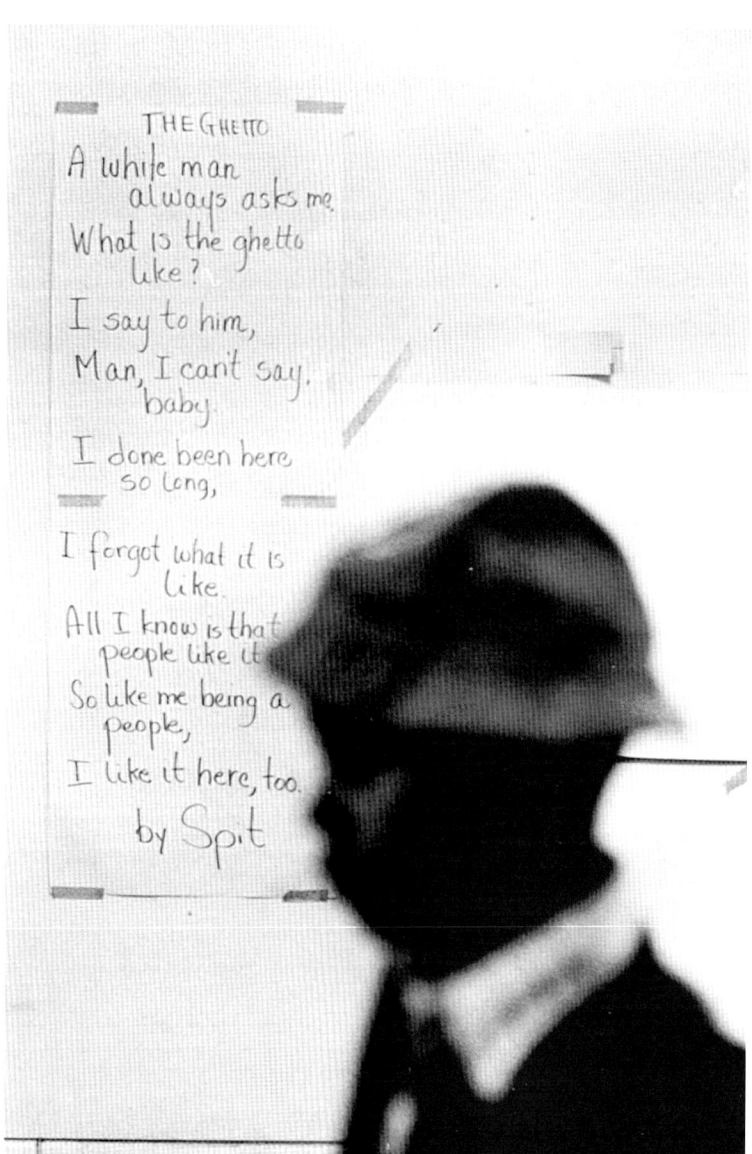

[The ghetto poem, *Poverty in Washington, DC Project*.]
ca. 1970
Digital print

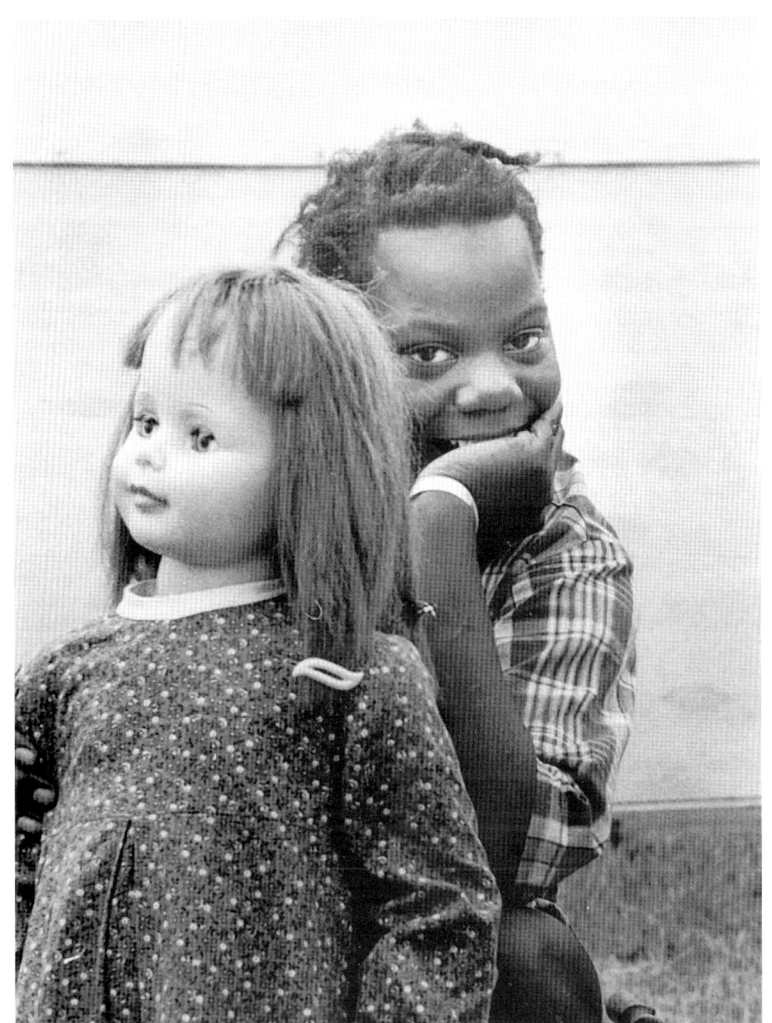

[Girl with doll, *Poverty in Washington, DC Project*.]
ca. 1970

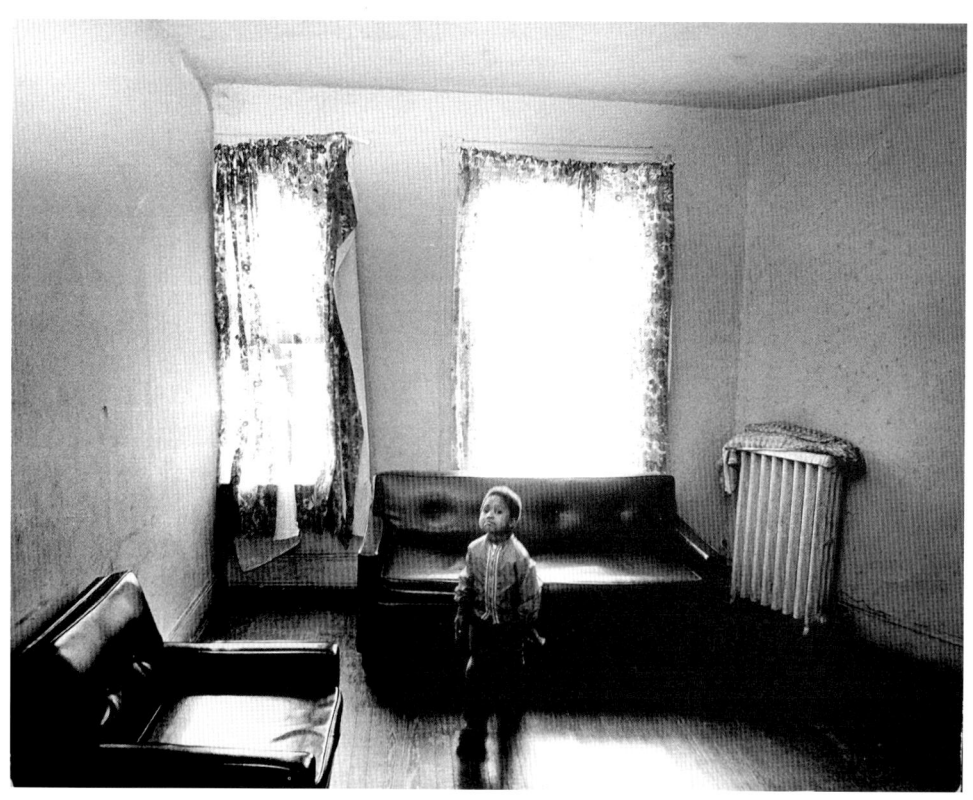

[Child, slum housing, *Poverty in Washington, DC Project.*]
ca. 1970

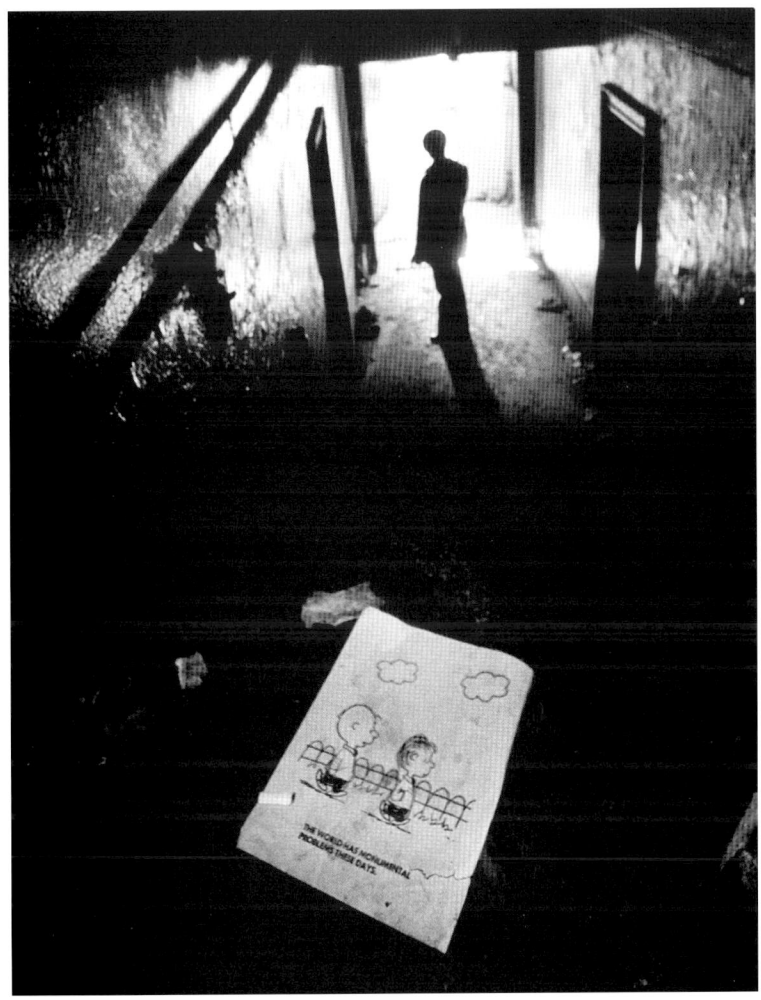

[Slum housing, *Poverty in Washington, DC Project*.] ca. 1970

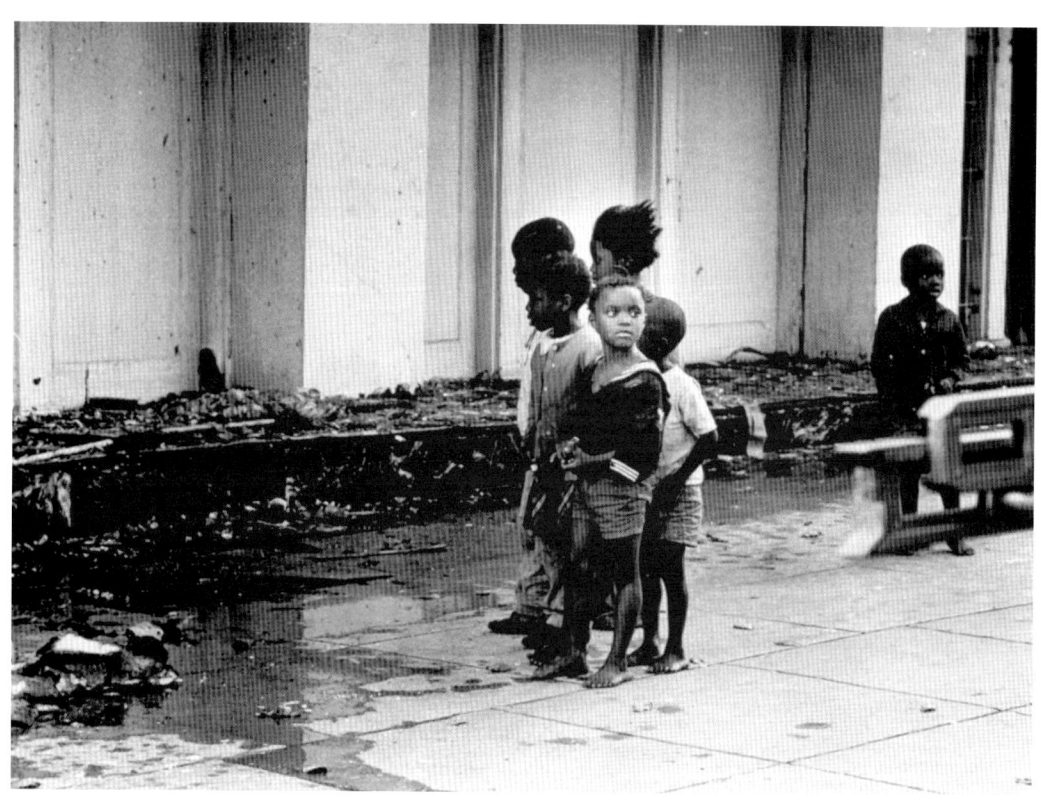

[Children, *Poverty in Washington, DC Project*.]
ca. 1970

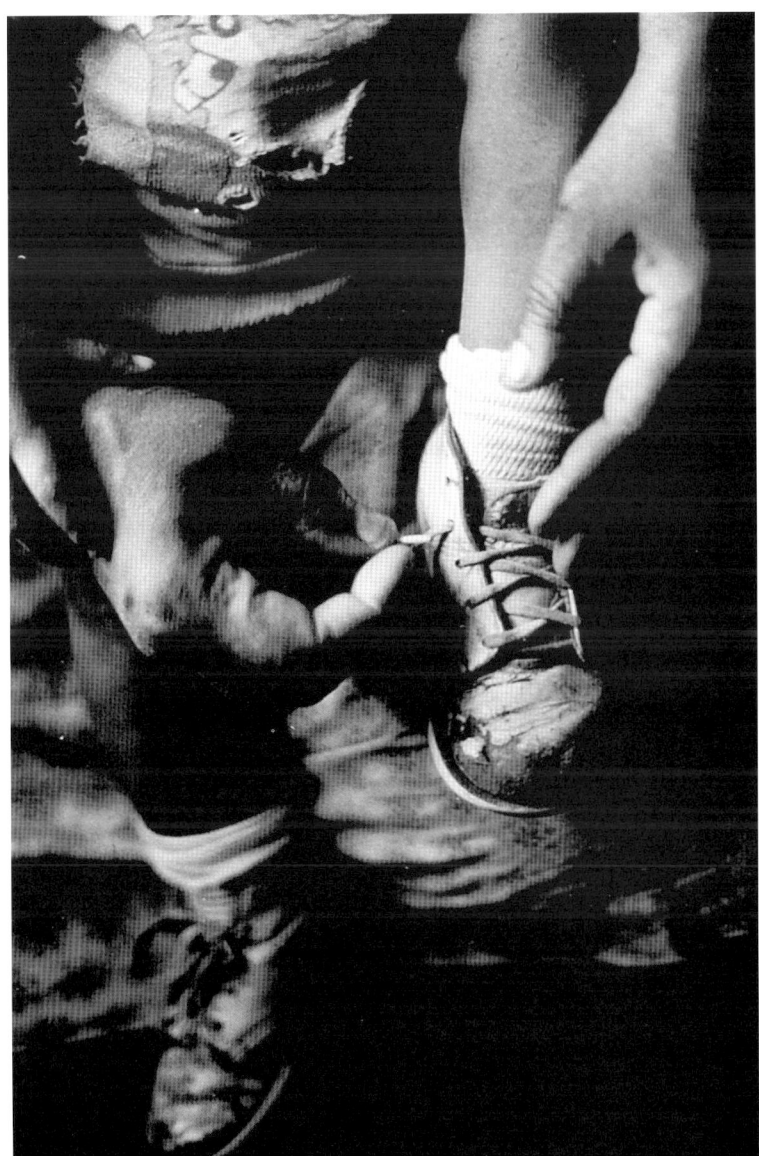

[Tying a shoelace, *Poverty in Washington, DC Project.*]
ca. 1970

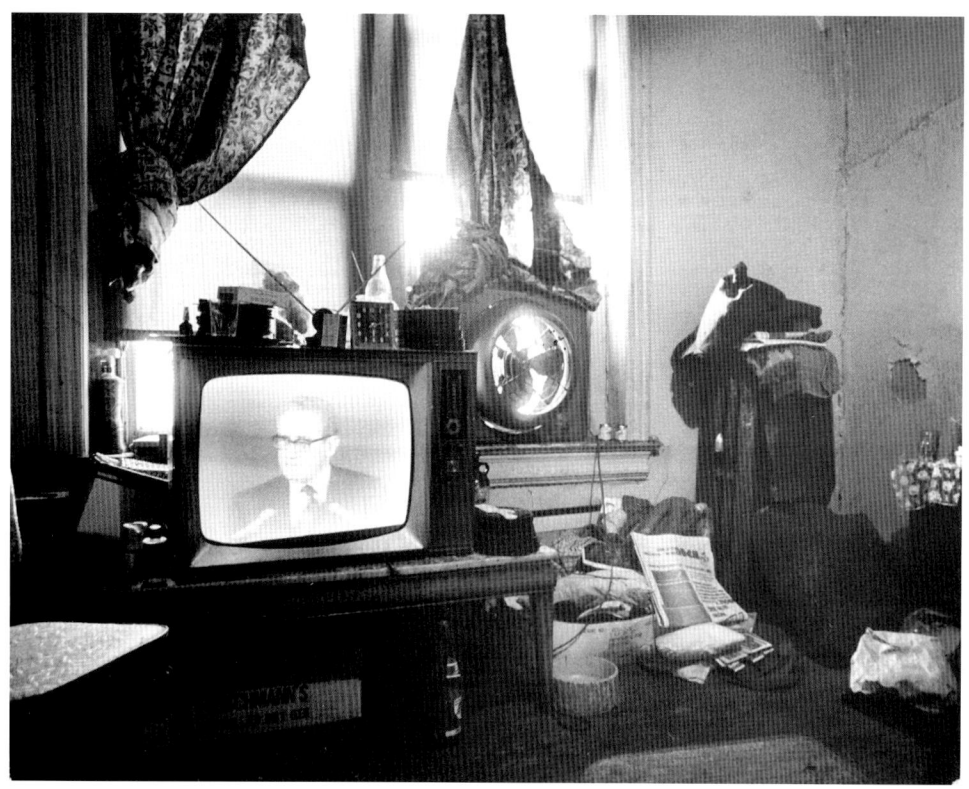

[Henry Kissinger, slum housing,
Poverty in Washington, DC Project.]
ca. 1970s

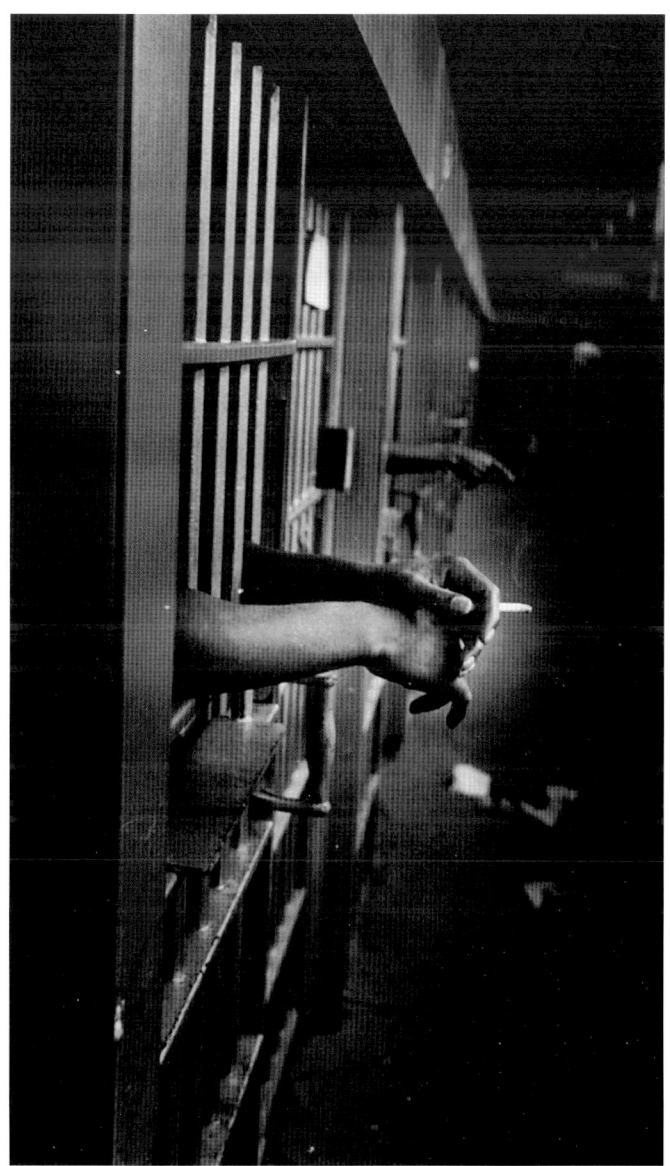

[Prison, *Poverty in Washington, DC Project.*]
ca. 1970
Digital print

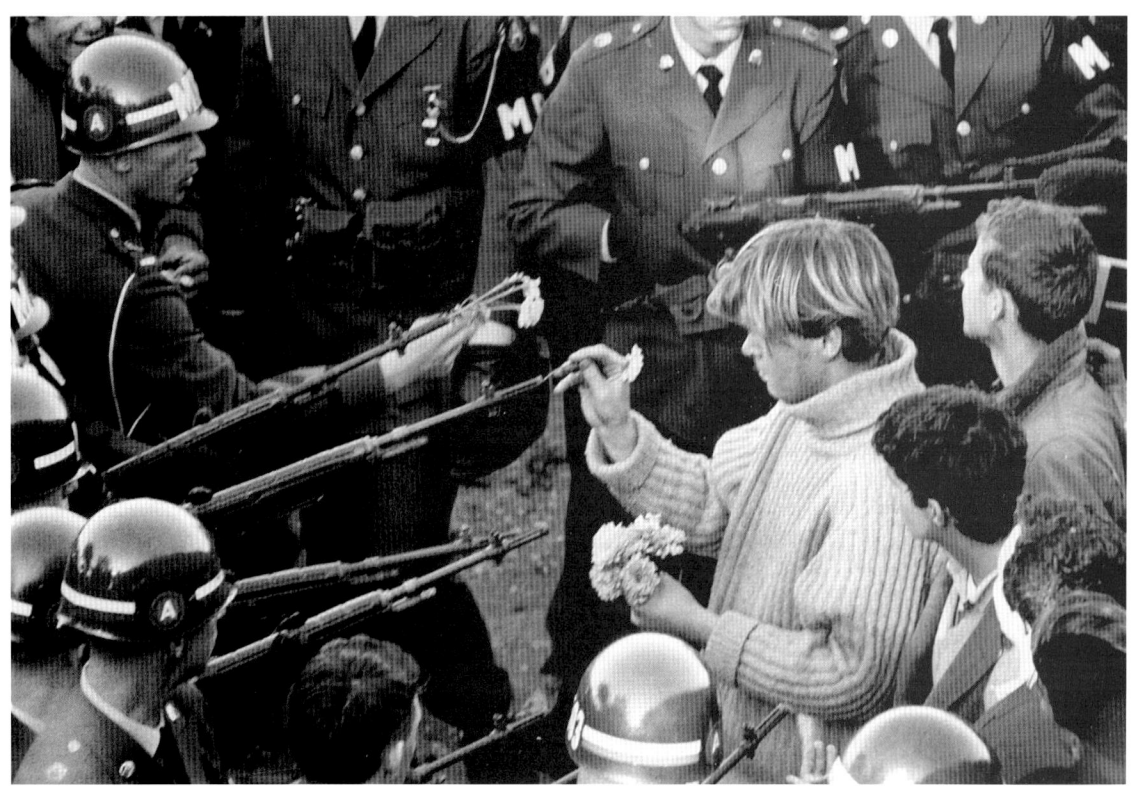

Flower Power
[Anti-Vietnam War demonstration at
the Pentagon, Washington, DC.]
1967

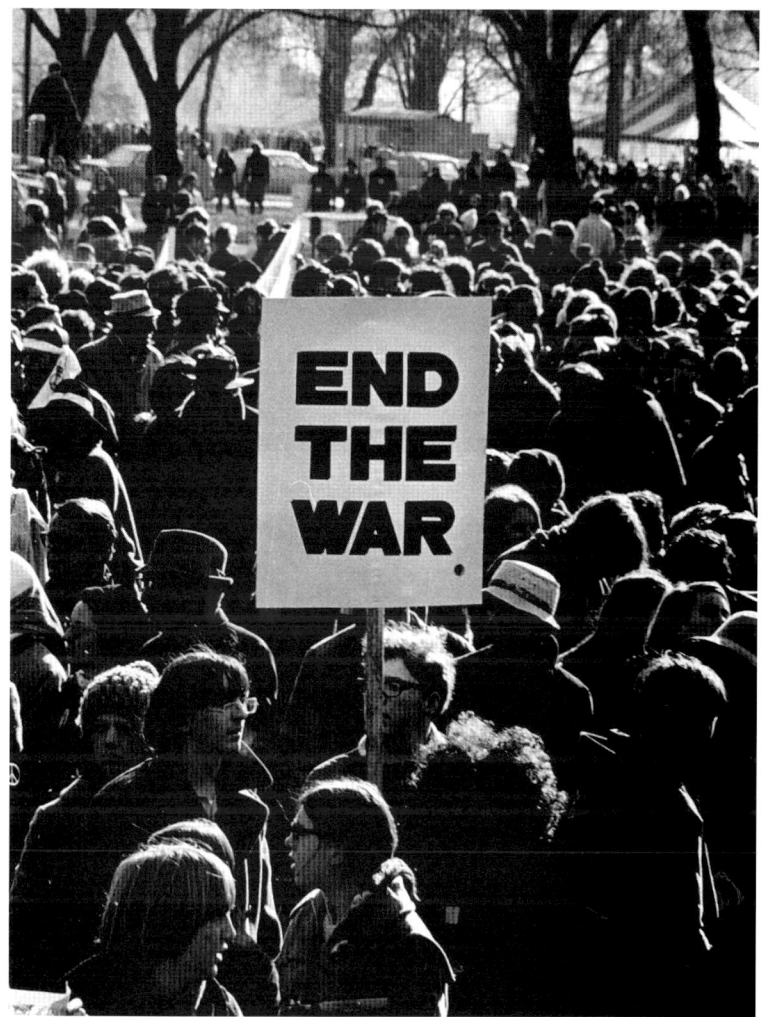

[End the War sign, anti-
Vietnam War demonstration,
Washington, DC.]
1968

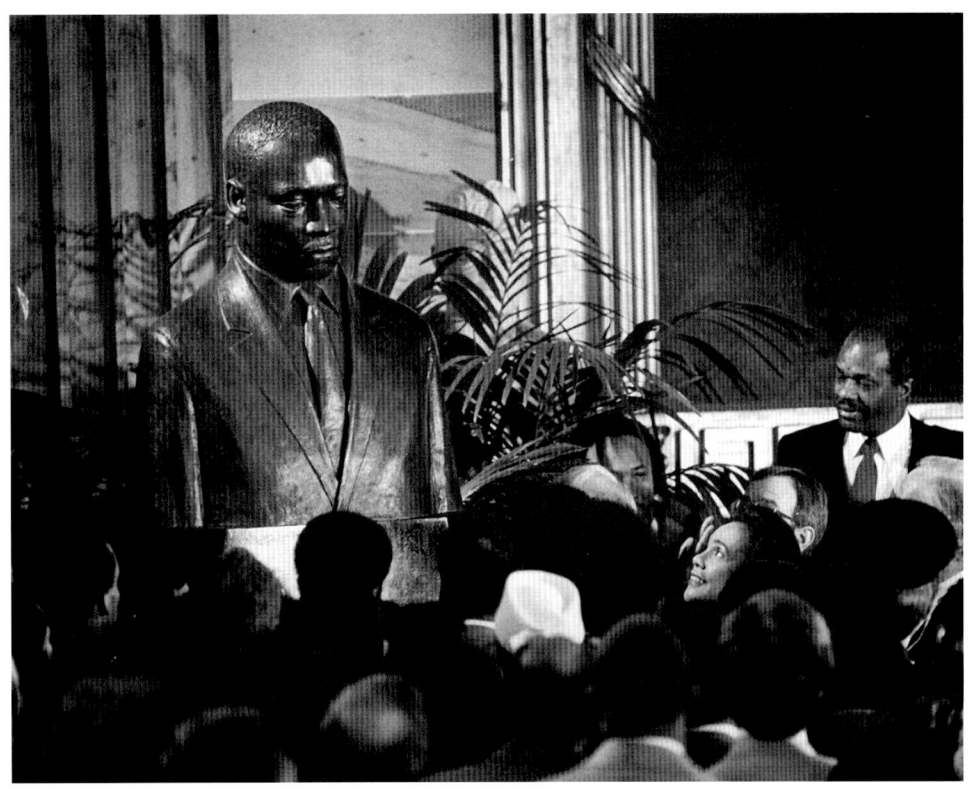

[Coretta Scott King at unveiling of her
late husband's bust in U.S. Capitol
Rotunda.]
1987

THE NATIONAL STAGE

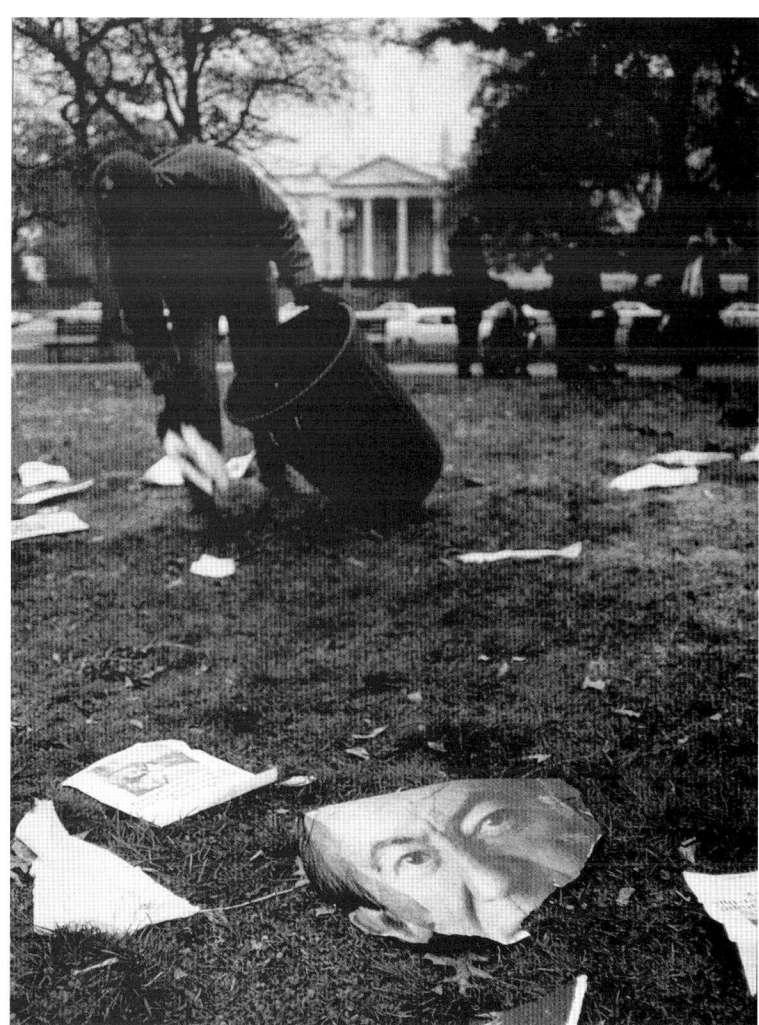

Election Day Aftermath
1968
Gelatin silver print on board

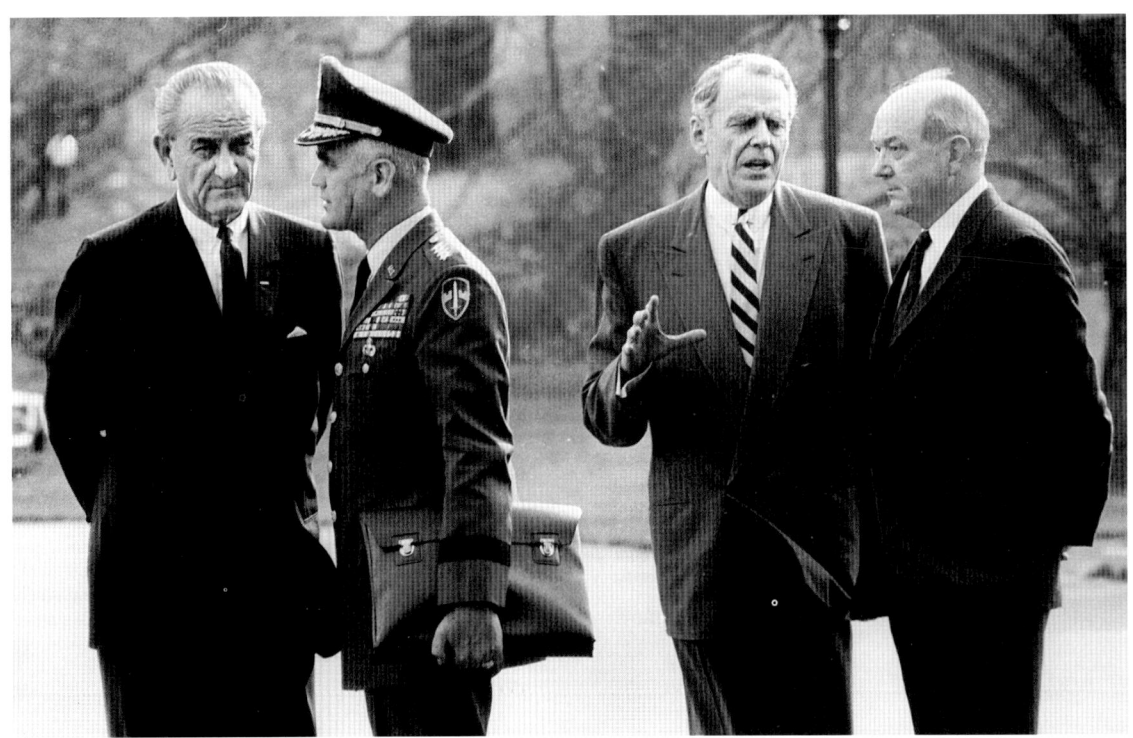

[President Lyndon Johnson, Chief of
Staff General William Westmoreland,
Secretary of Defense Clifford Clark
(who had recently replaced Robert
McNamara), and Secretary of State
Dean Rusk.]
1968

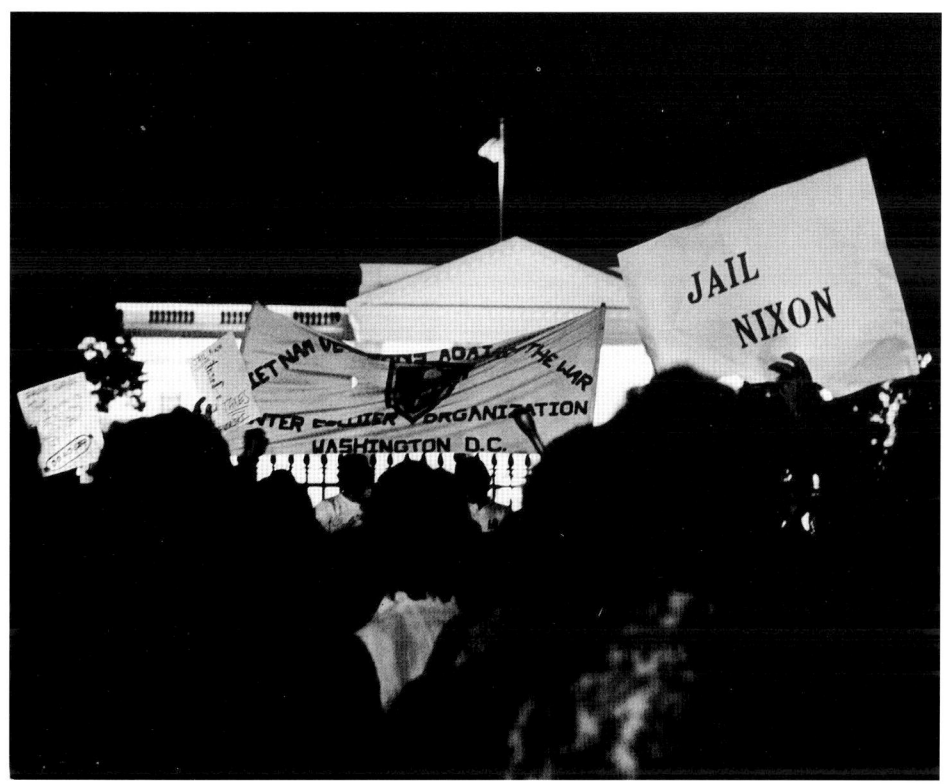

Crowds gathered outside the White
House as then President Nixon tells
the American public via television he
is going to resign.
1974

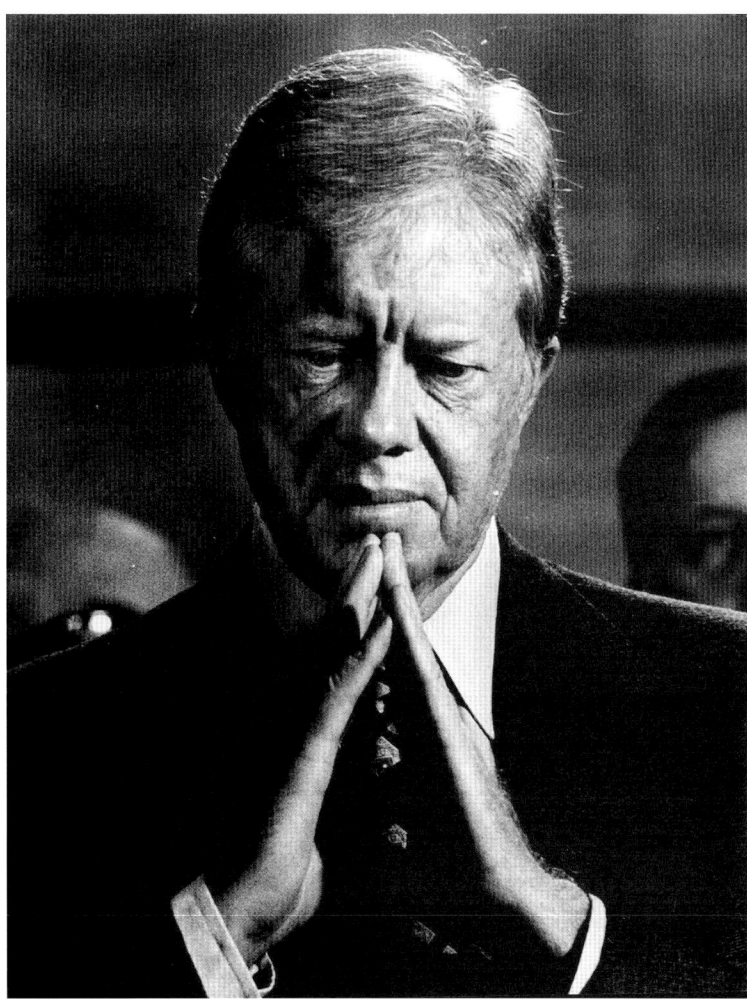

[President Jimmy Carter in contemplation.]
late 1970s

BERNIE BOSTON

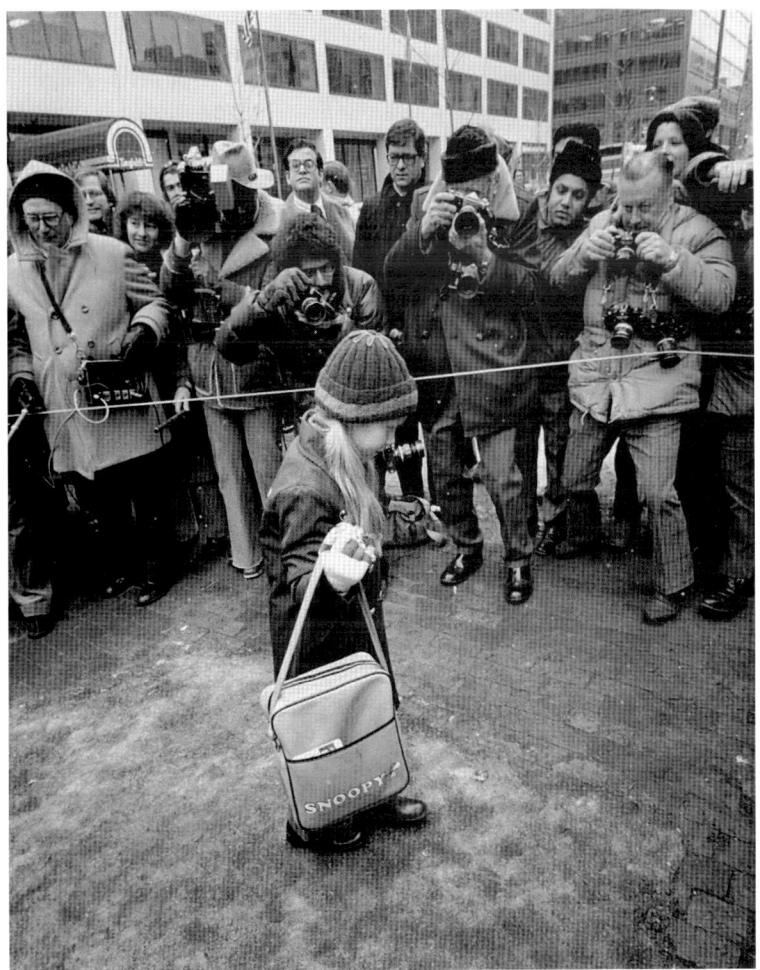

[Amy Carter goes to school
while reporters look on.]
1977

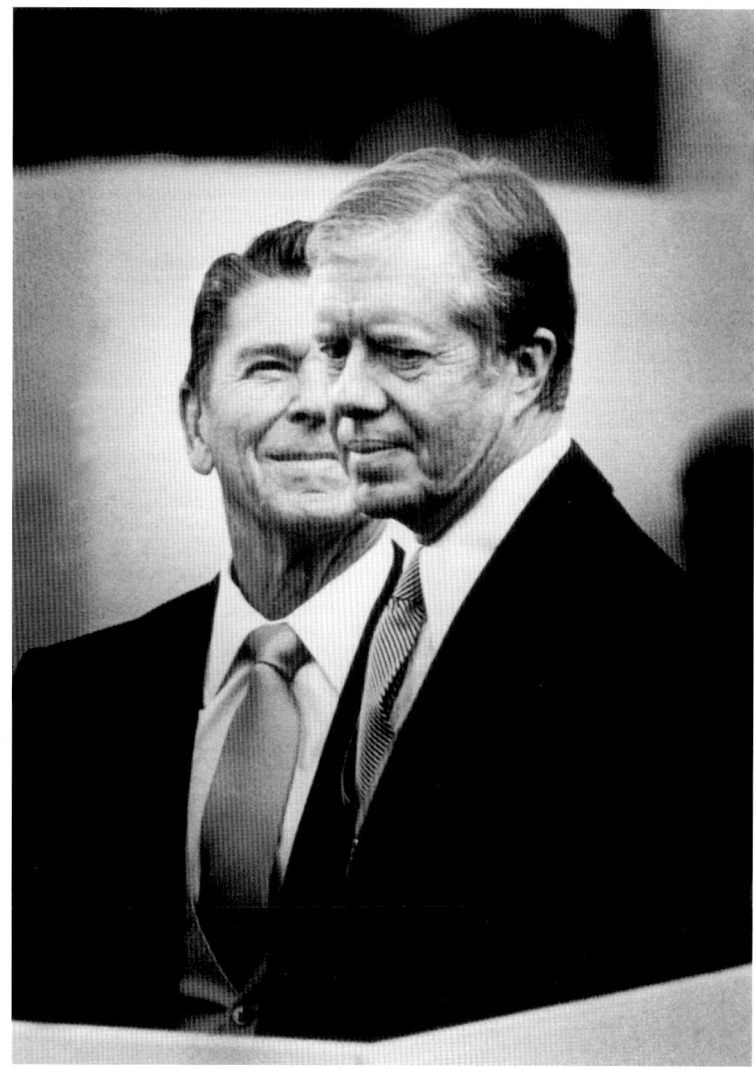

[President Jimmy Carter with
President-elect Ronald Reagan
at Reagan's Inauguration.]
1981

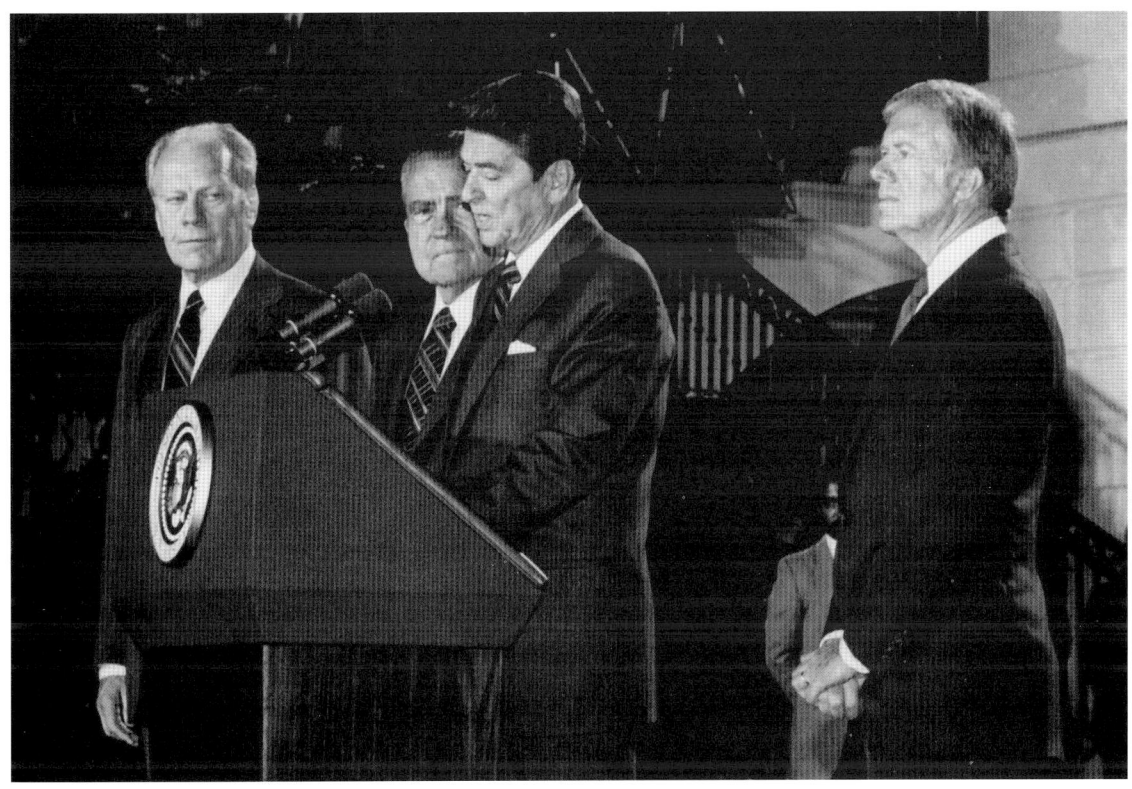

[Four American presidents: (l. to r.)
Gerald Ford, Richard Nixon,
Ronald Reagan, and Jimmy Carter.]
1981
Digital print
Los Angeles Times Photo
by Bernie Boston

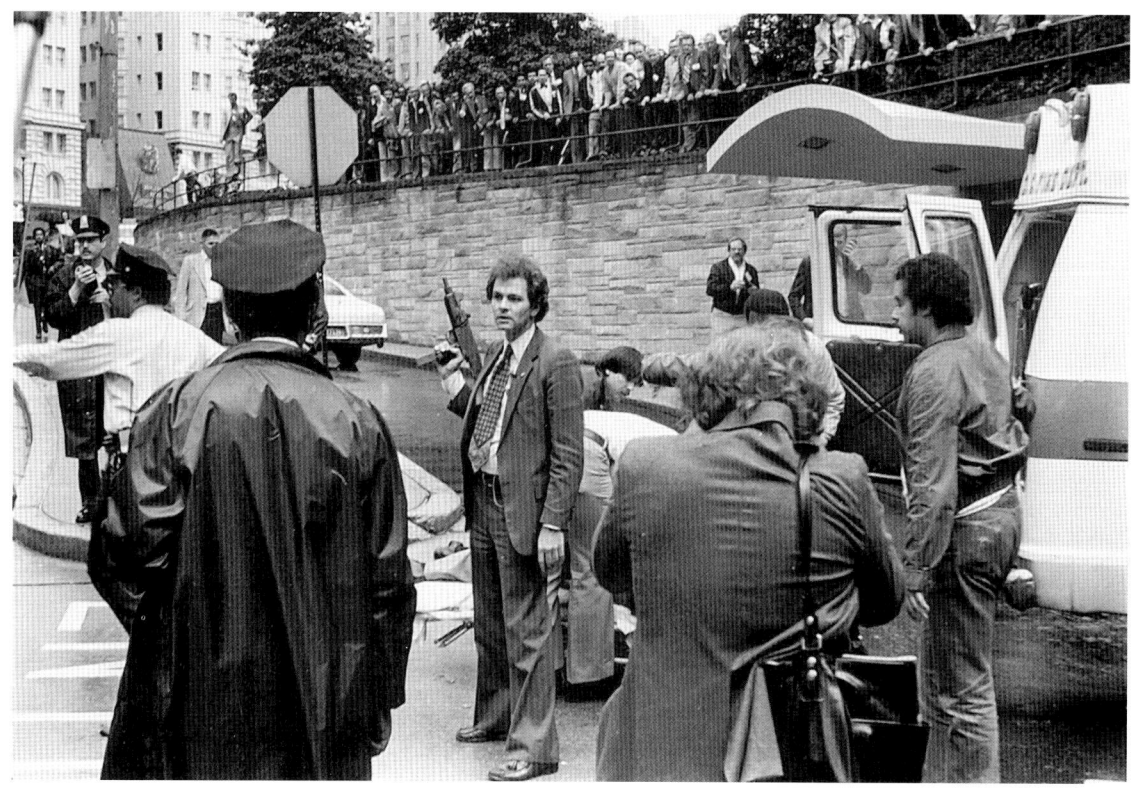

[An injured James Brady is placed in
an ambulance after being shot during
an assasination attempt on President
Reagan, March 30, 1981.]
1981

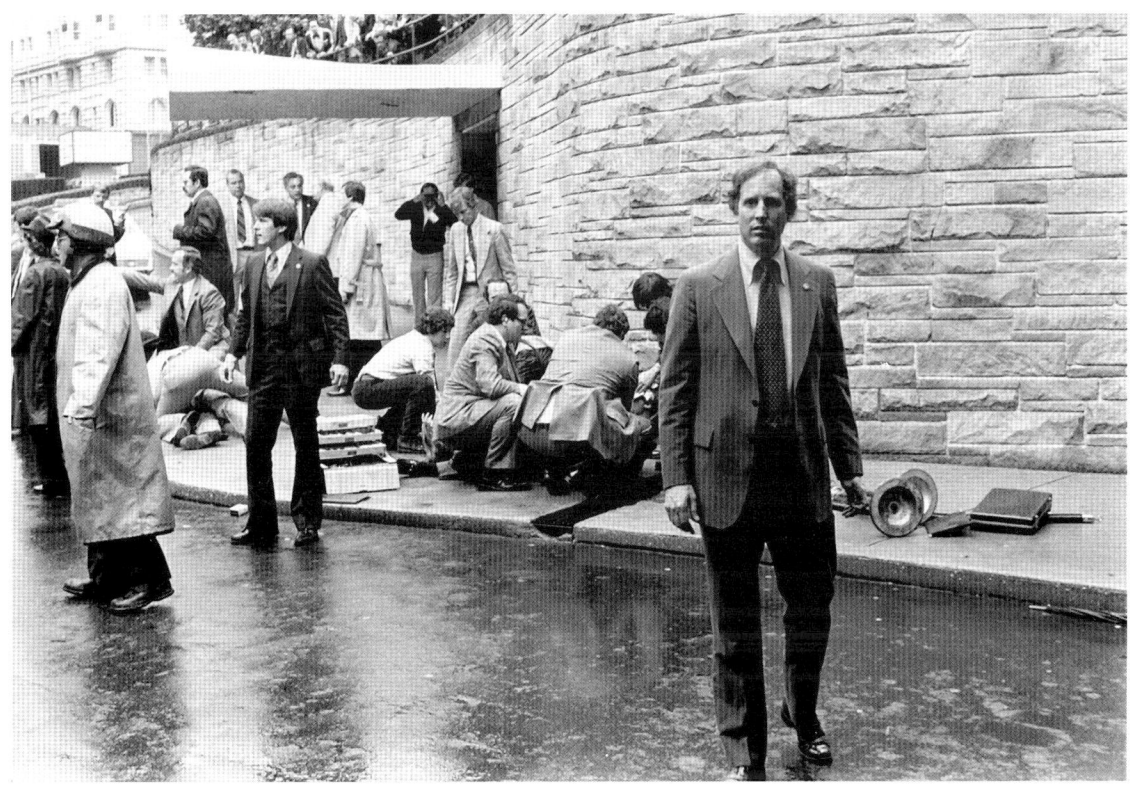

[Secret Service members tend to the
gunshot wounds of James Brady,
March 30, 1981.]
1981

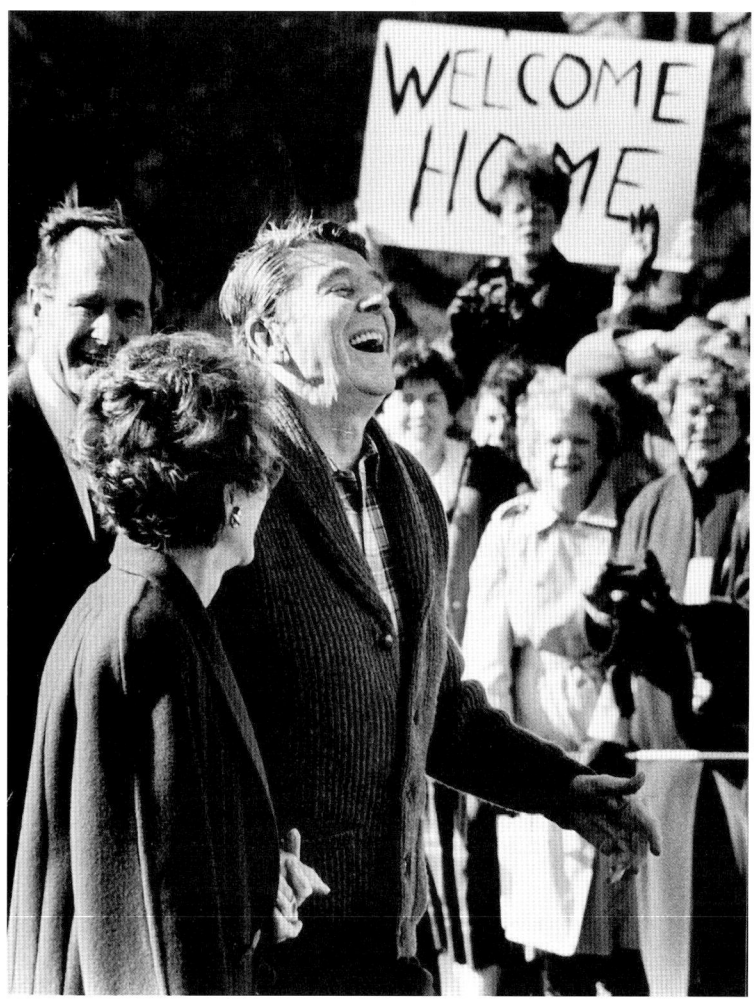

Welcome Home
President Reagan returns to
White House after surgery.
1981

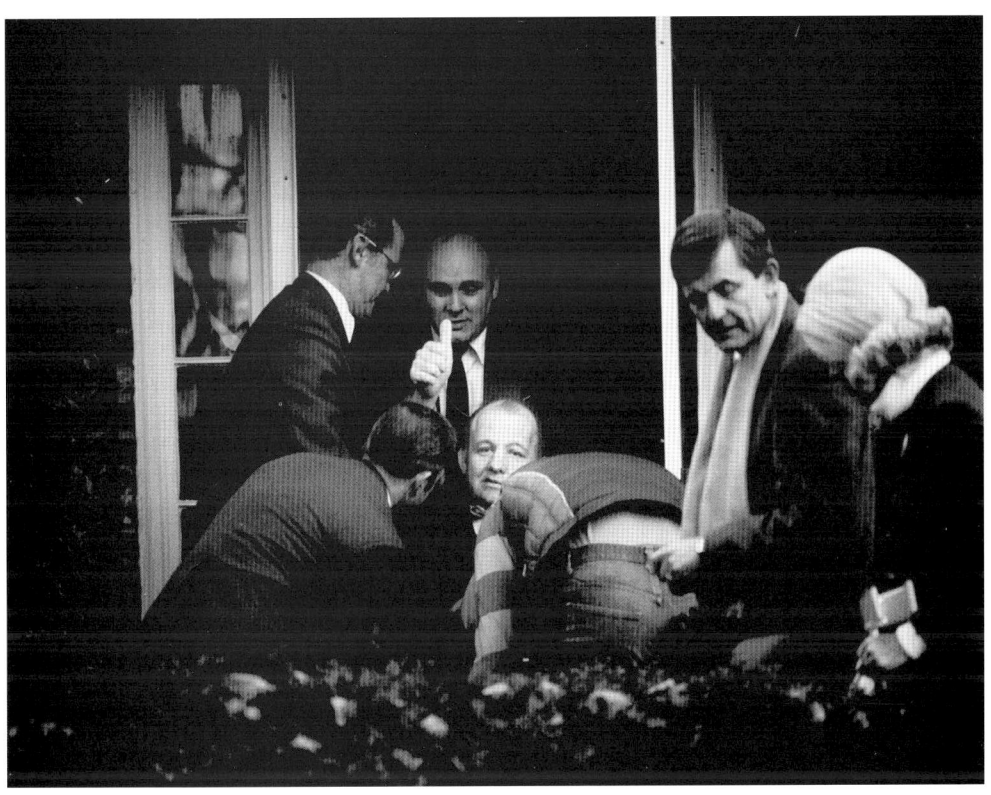

[James Brady returns home
from hospital.]
1981

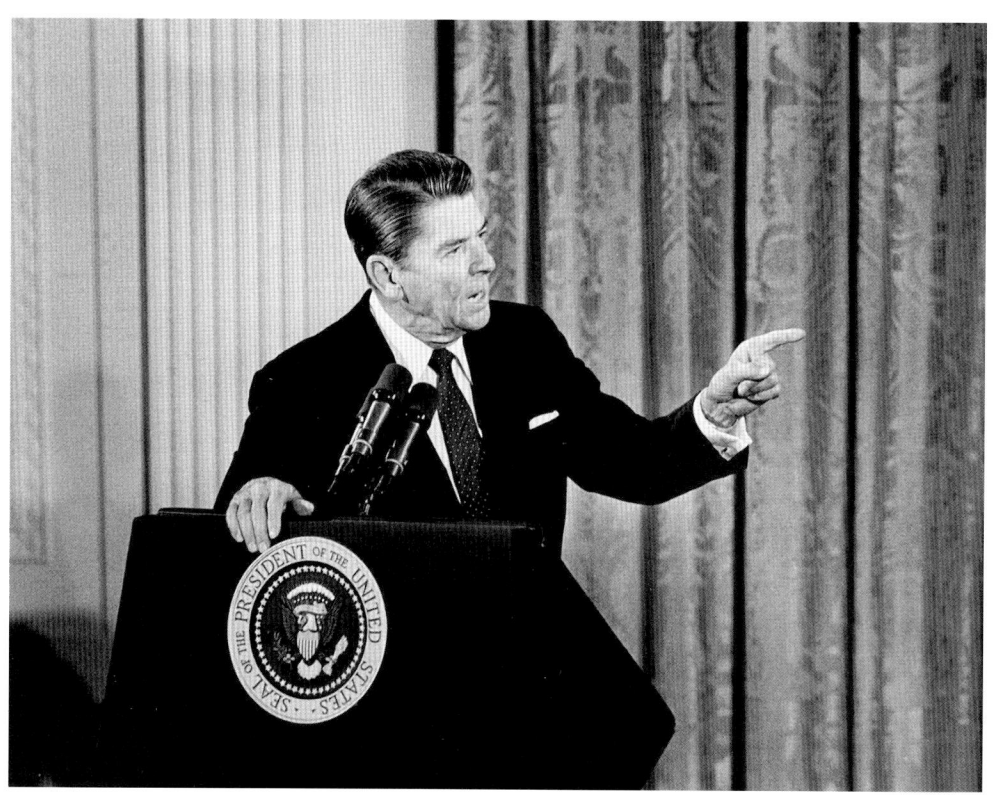

"Shut Up."
President Ronald Reagan yells "shut
up!" to Republican candidate Richard
Arnold of California, who interrupted
Reagan's speech, October 6, 1982
1982
Los Angeles Times Photo
by Bernie Boston

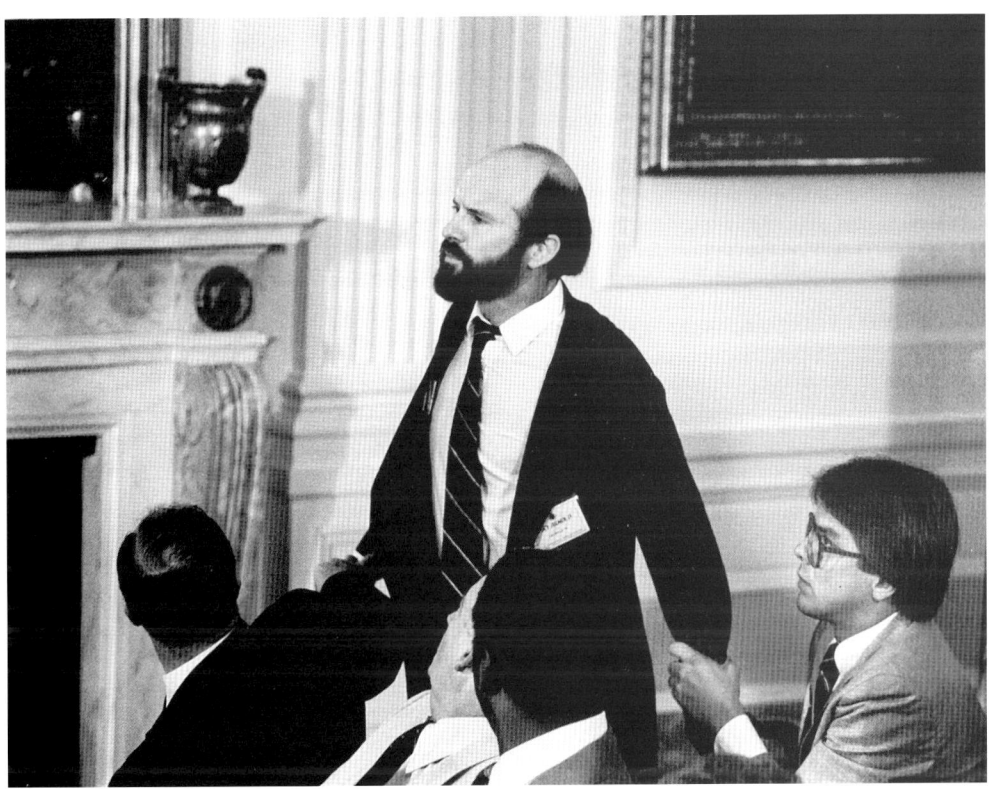

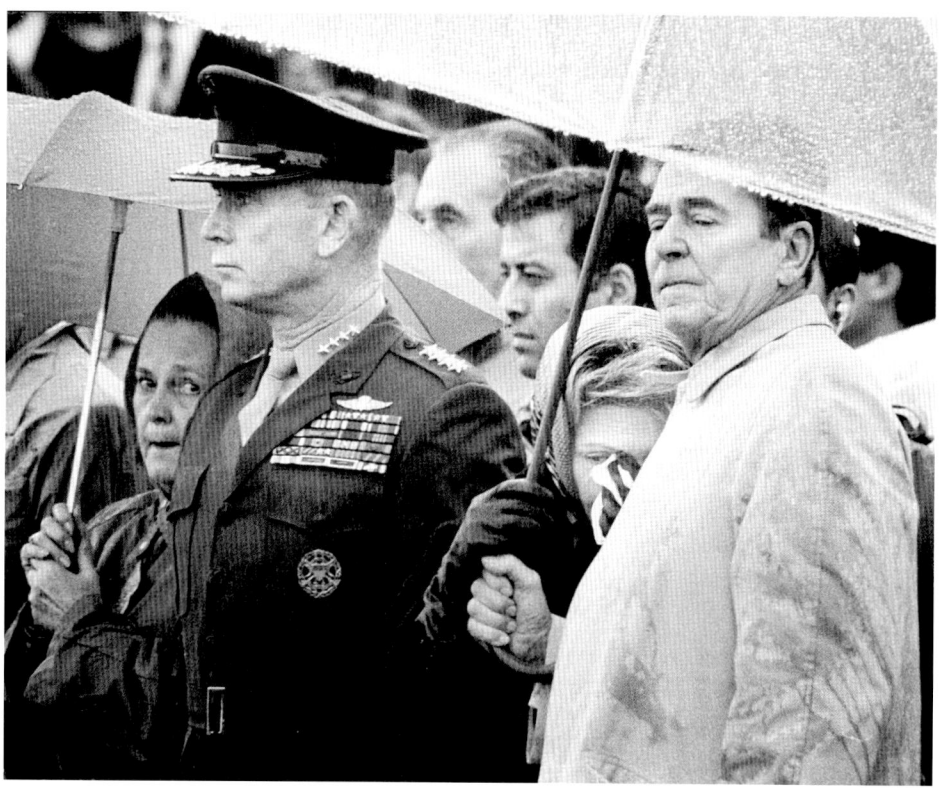

A Tear for the Dead
President and Mrs. Reagan attend
memorial services for U.S.
marines killed in attack on barracks in
Lebanon—Mrs. Reagan wipes a tear.
1983
Los Angeles Times Photo
by Bernie Boston

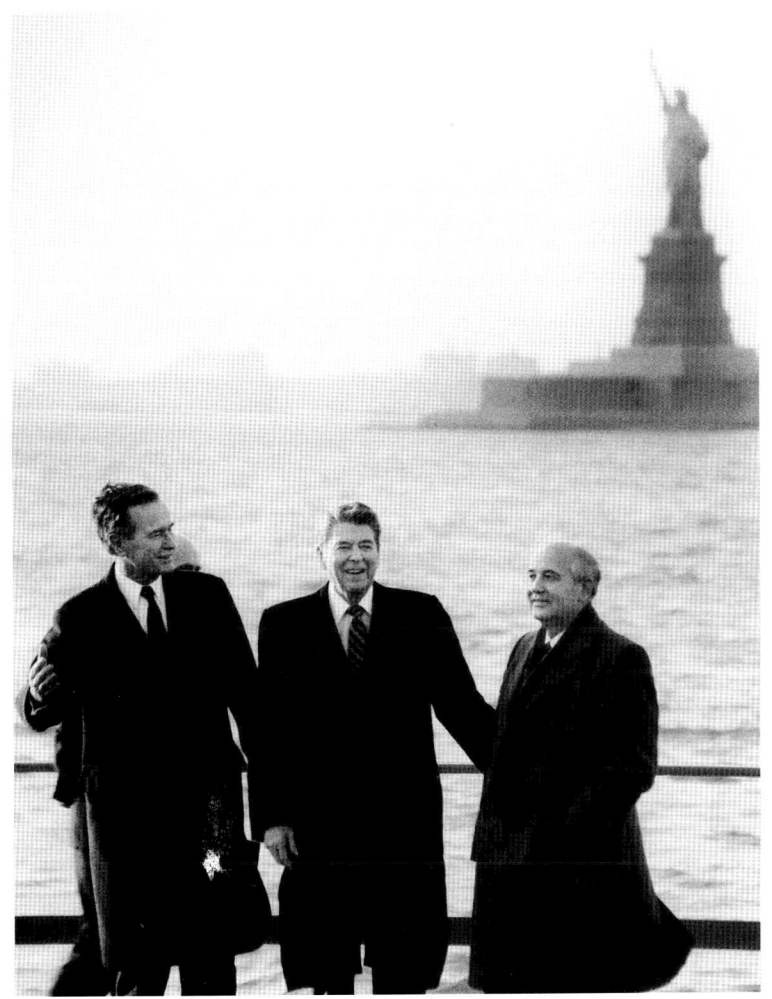

[Vice President Bush, President Reagan, and Soviet Union Leader Mikhail Gorbachev with the Statue of Liberty in the background.]
1987
Los Angeles Times Photo
by Bernie Boston

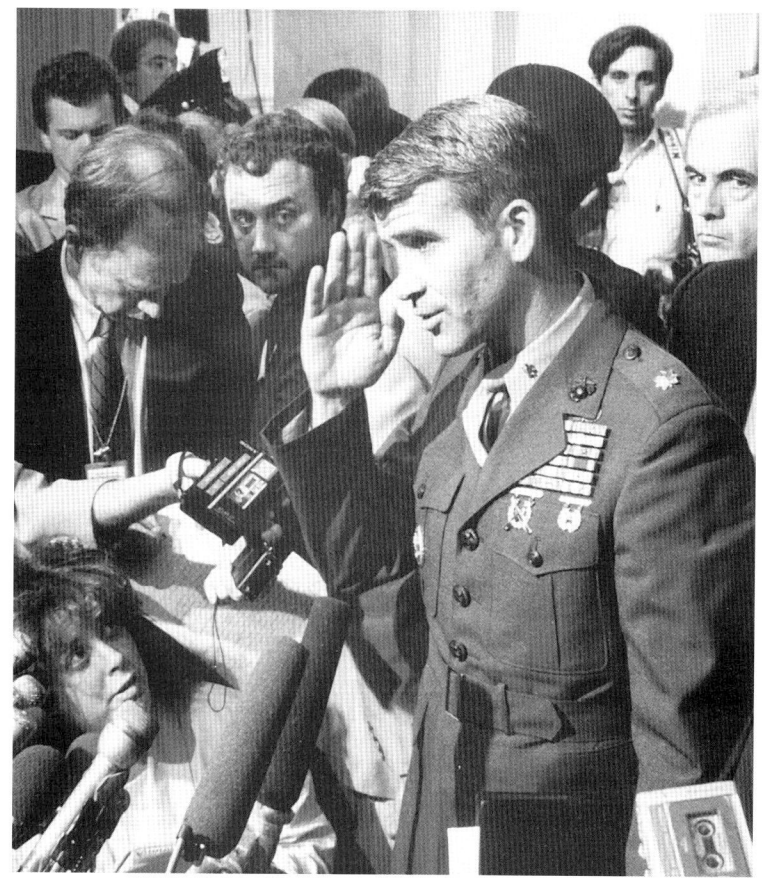

Washington DC, 14 July 87.
Iran-Contra Hearings. Lt Col.
Oliver North salutes the press
and cameras outside the caucus
room at the end of his six days
of testimony befor [sic] the Iran
Contra Joint Committee.
1987
News wire photo with caption

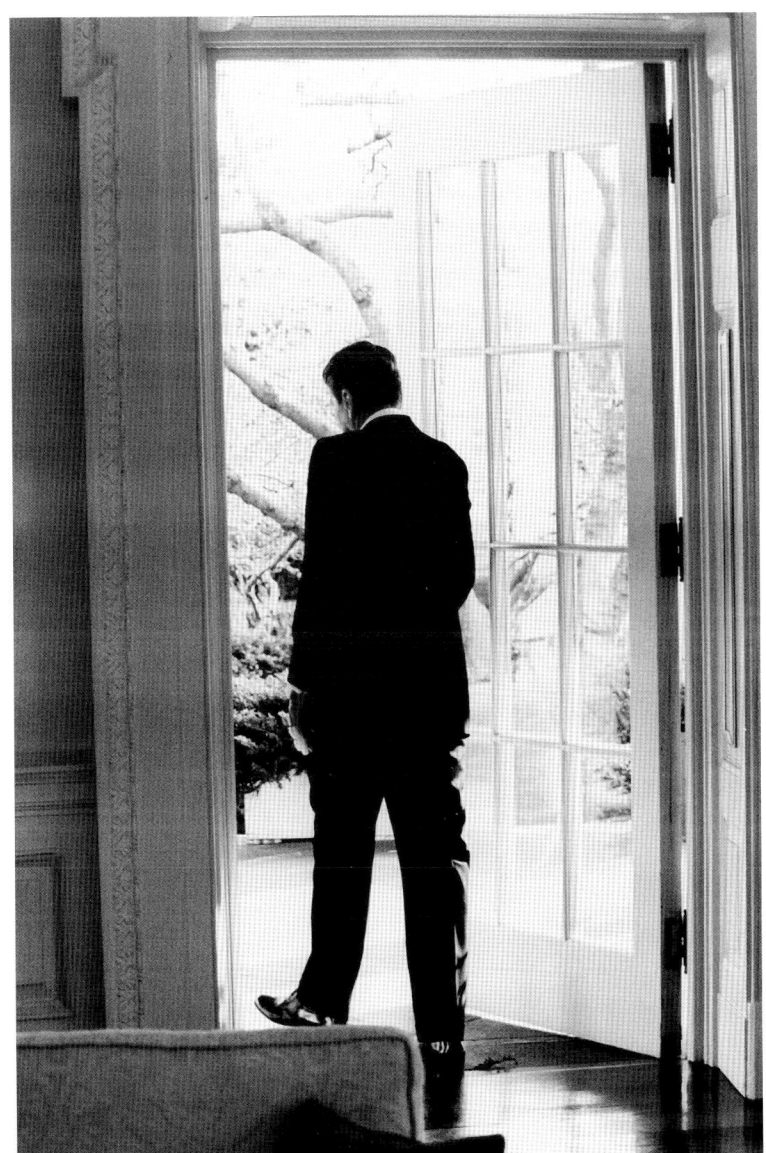

[President Ronald Reagan leaves
the White House at the end of
his two terms in office.]
1989

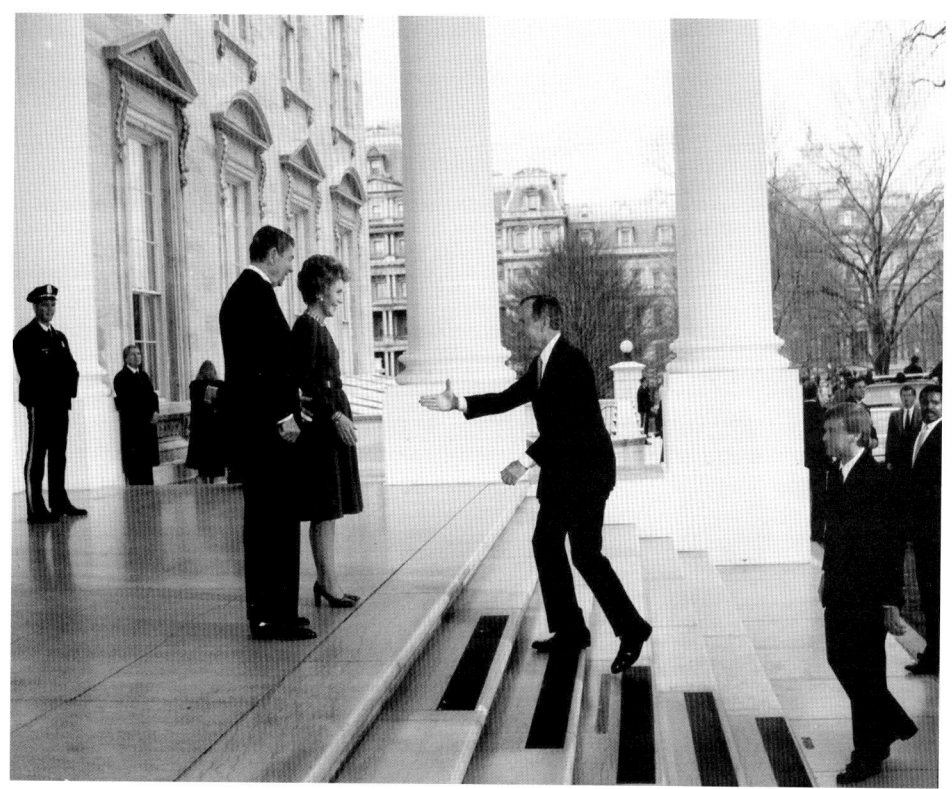

[President-elect George Bush and
Vice President Dan Quayle are
greeted on the White House steps by
President and Mrs. Reagan.]
1989

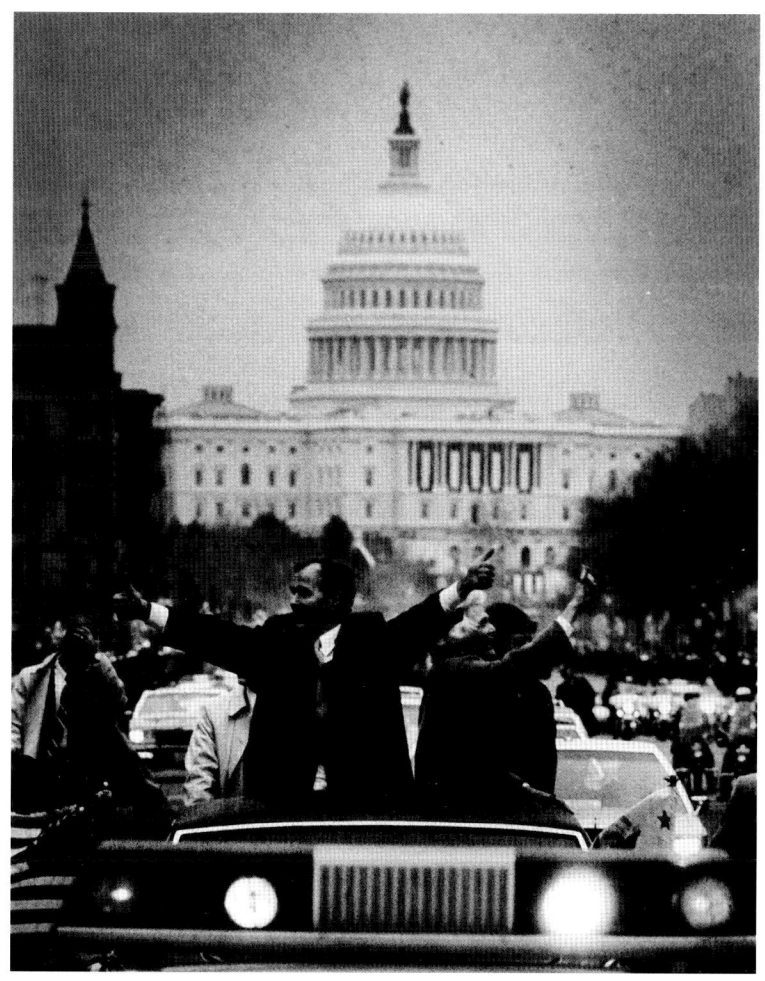

[President and Mrs. Bush greet
the public from their motorcade
during Inaugural events.]
1989

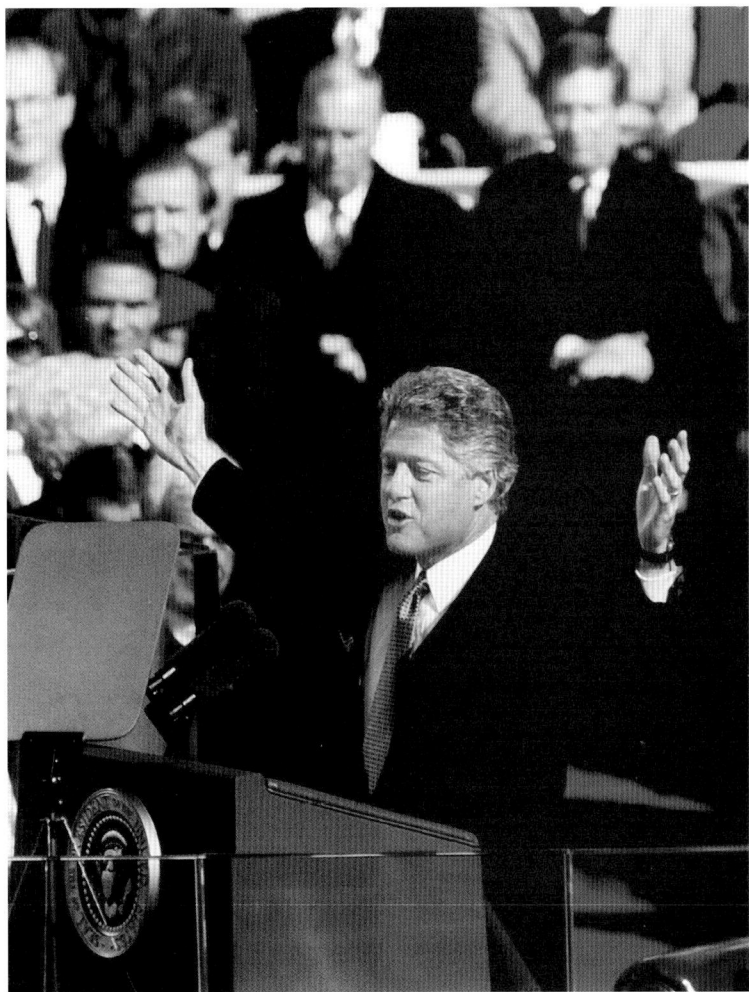

[President-elect William "Bill" Clinton speaks at his Inauguration ceremony.] 1993

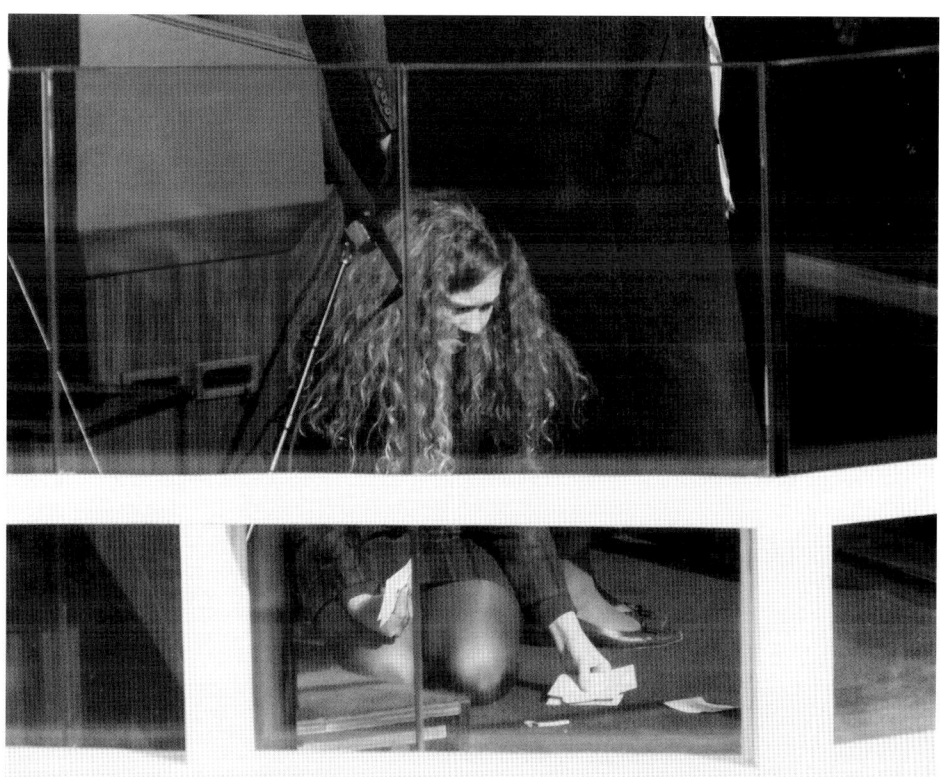

[Chelsea Clinton picks up her father's
Inaugural speech notes.]
1993

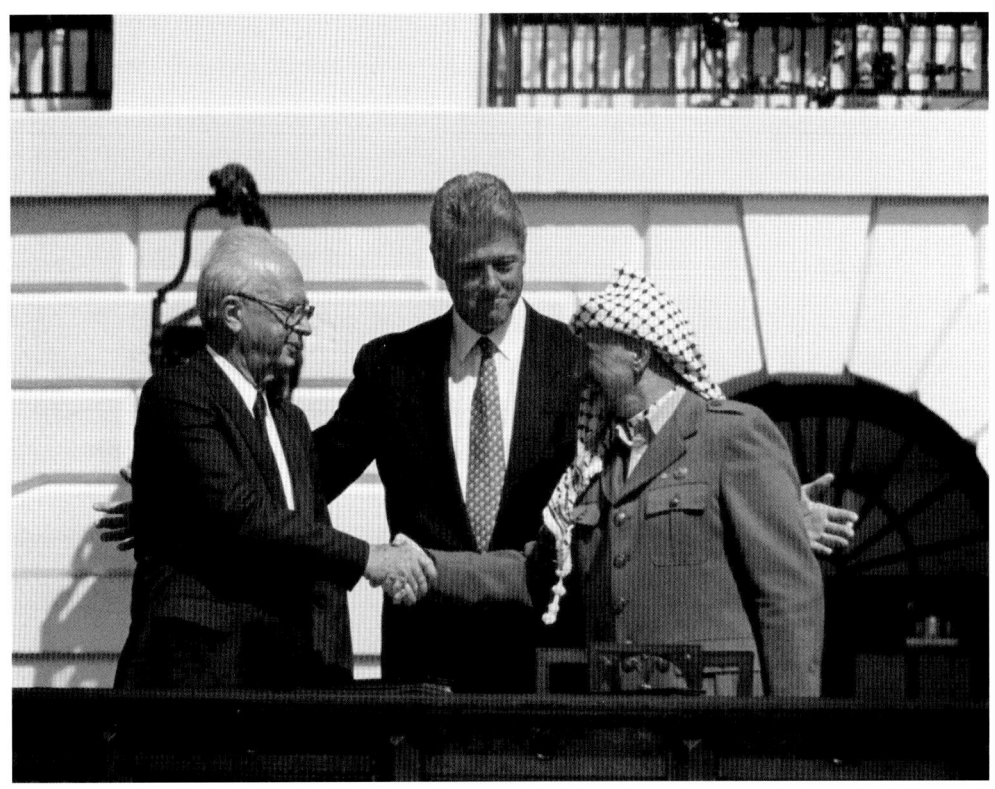

President Clinton looks on as
Israel's Yitzhak Rabin and PLO's
Yassar Arafat shake hands after
signing Middle East Peace Accord,
Oslo, Norway, September 13, 1993.
1993
Los Angeles Times Photo
by Bernie Boston

FEATURES AND PORTRAITS

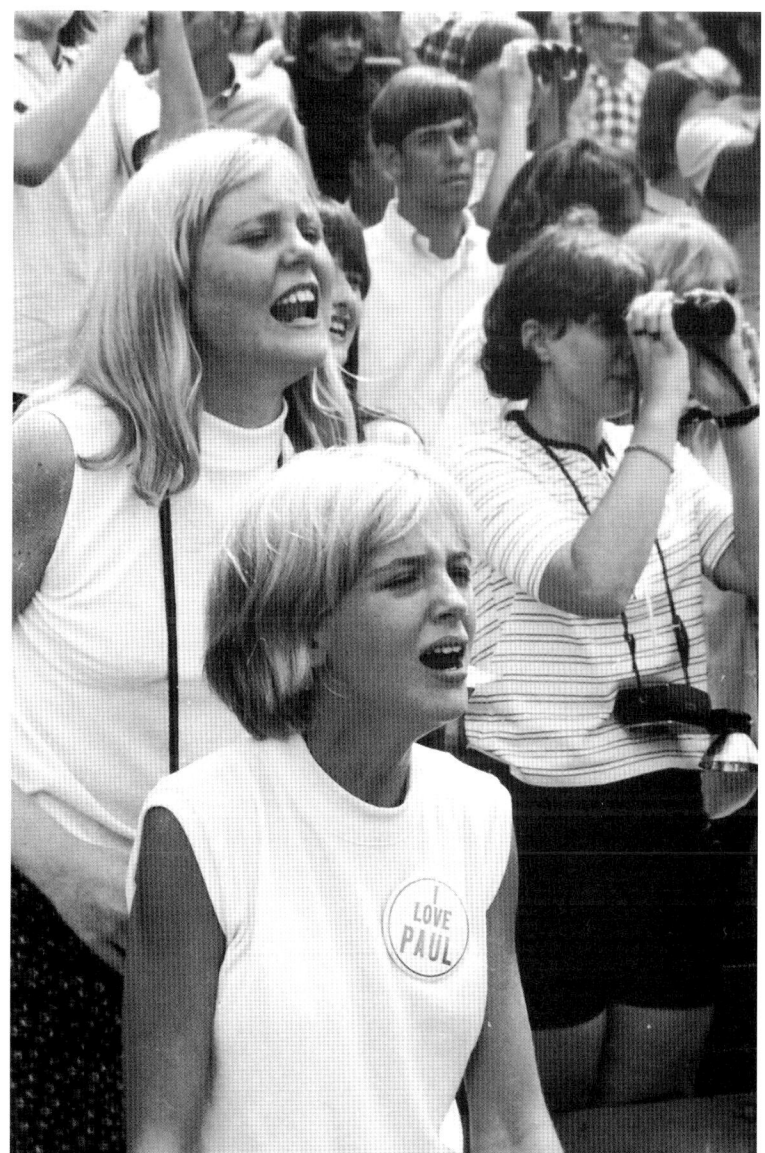

[Fans react to the Beatles' concert at Cincinnati Gardens during the Fab Four's first American tour and first trip to Cincinnati, OH, August 27, 1964.]
1964

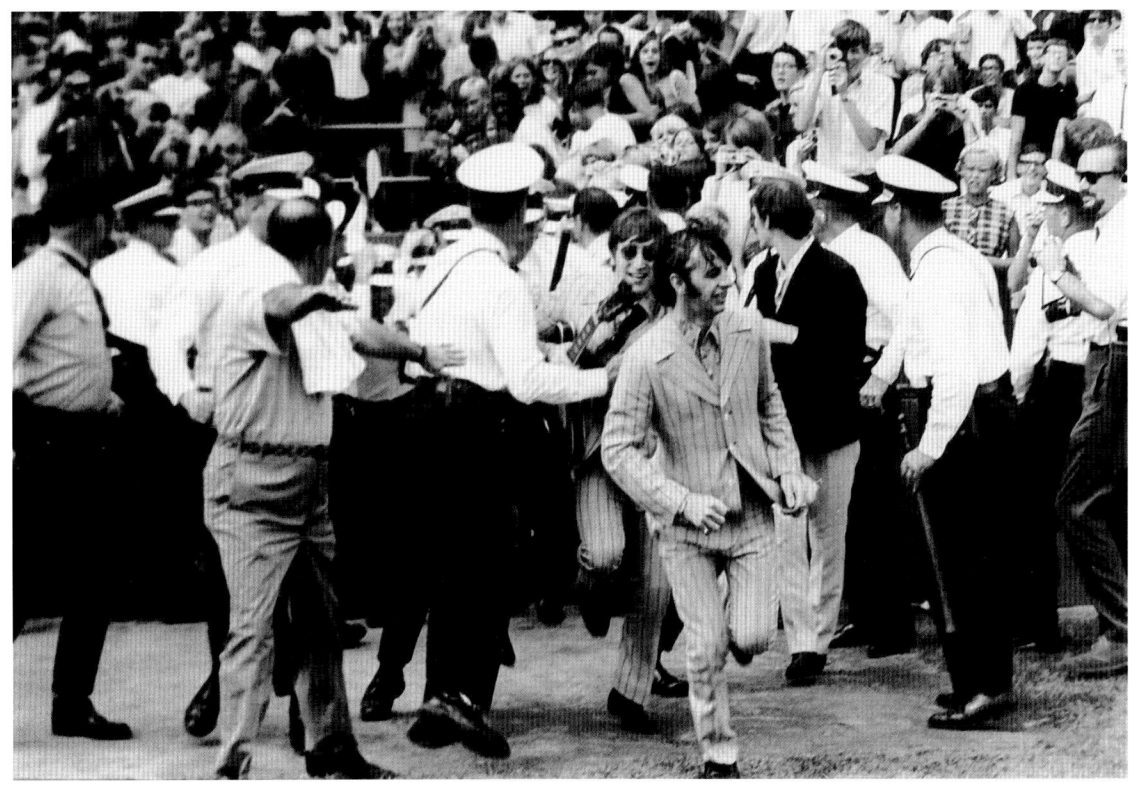

[John Lennon and Ringo Starr
emerge from a throng of fans.]
1964

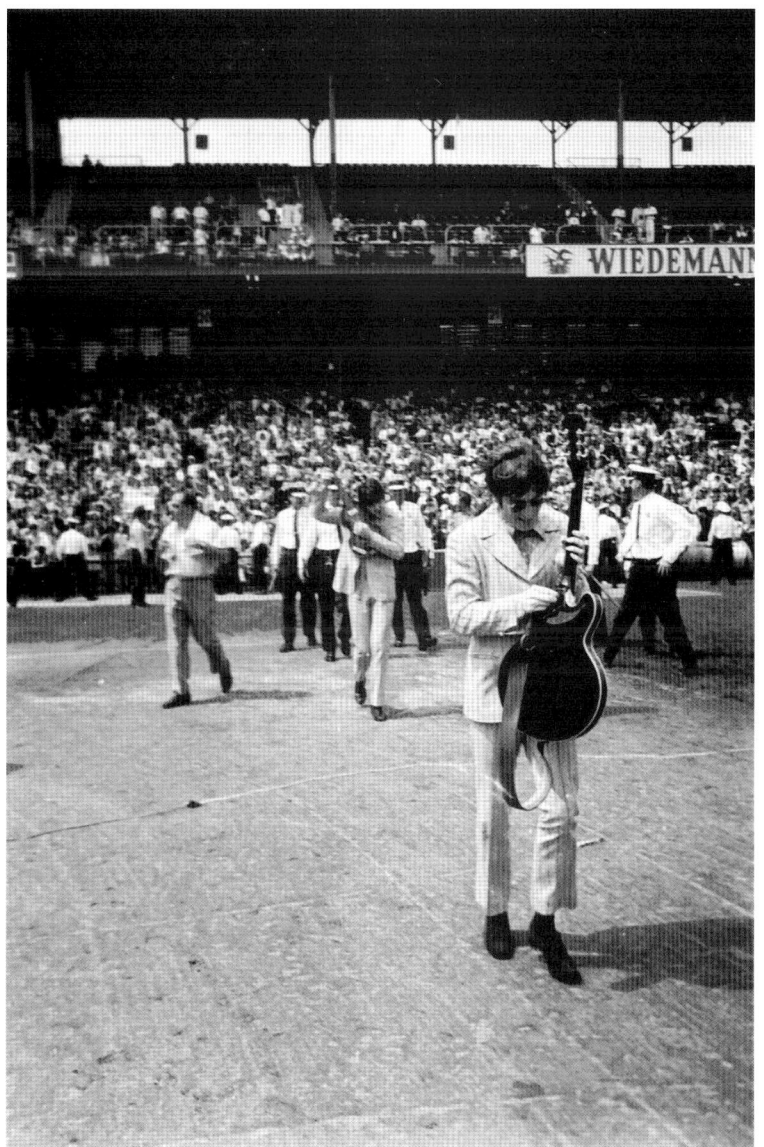

[John Lennon walks towards the stage at Cincinnati Gardens.] 1964

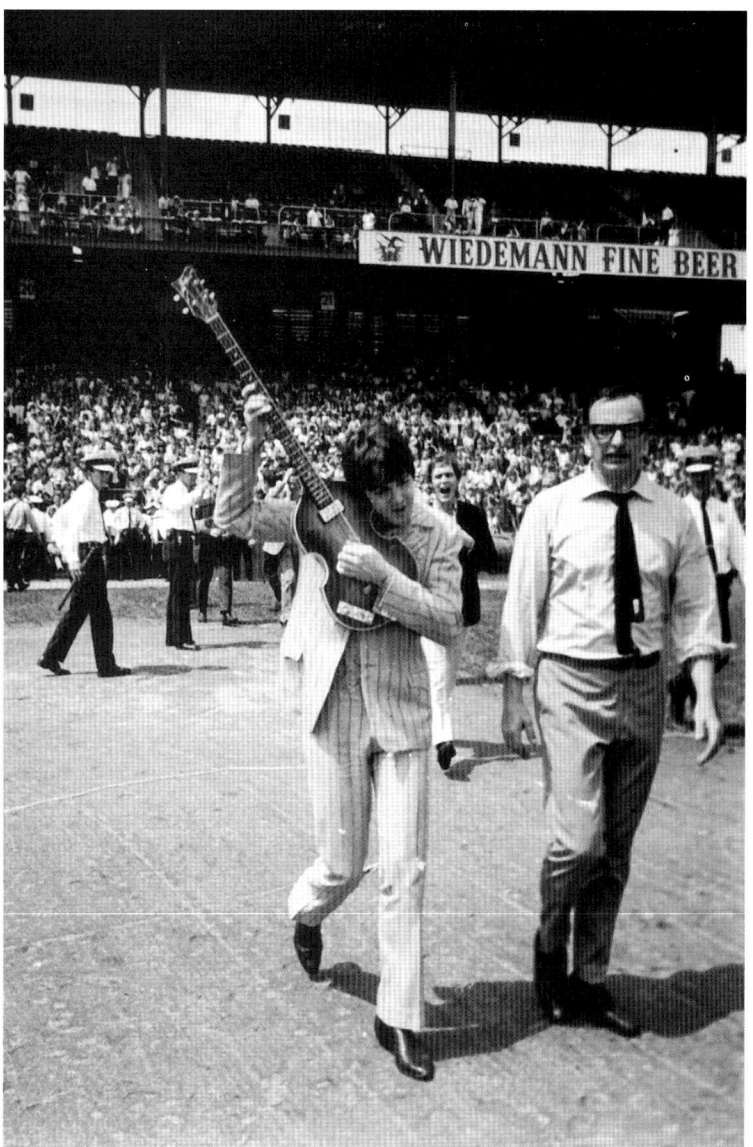

[Paul McCartney walks towards the stage at Cincinnati Gardens.] 1964

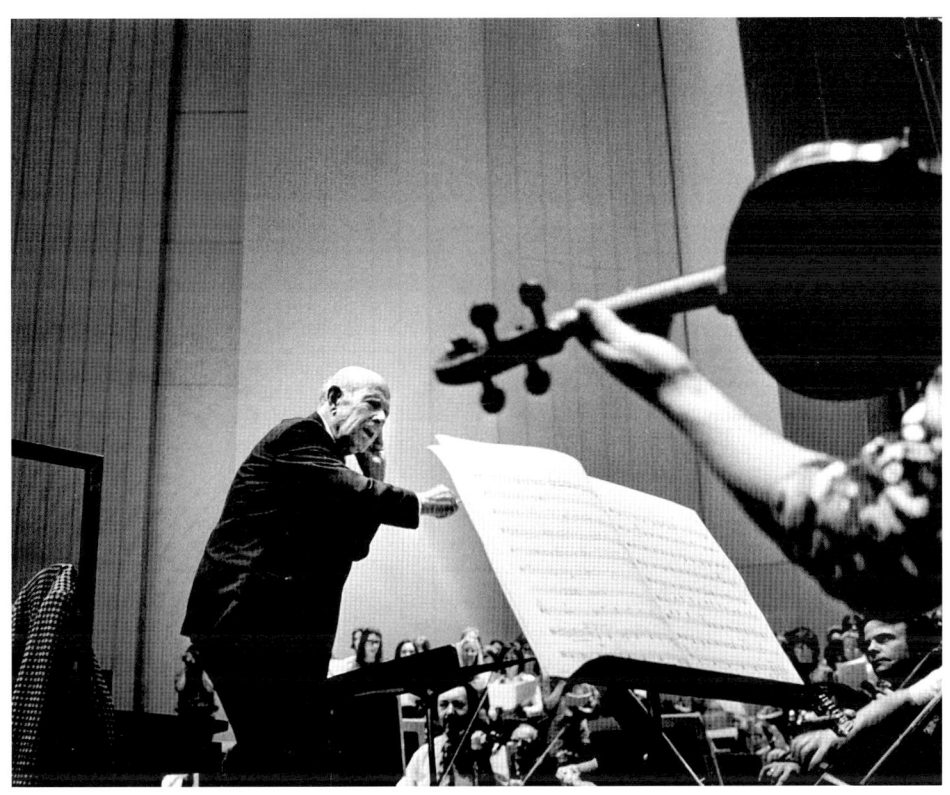

Pablo Casals during one of his
very last appearances conducts the
National Symphony Orchestra.
ca. 1972

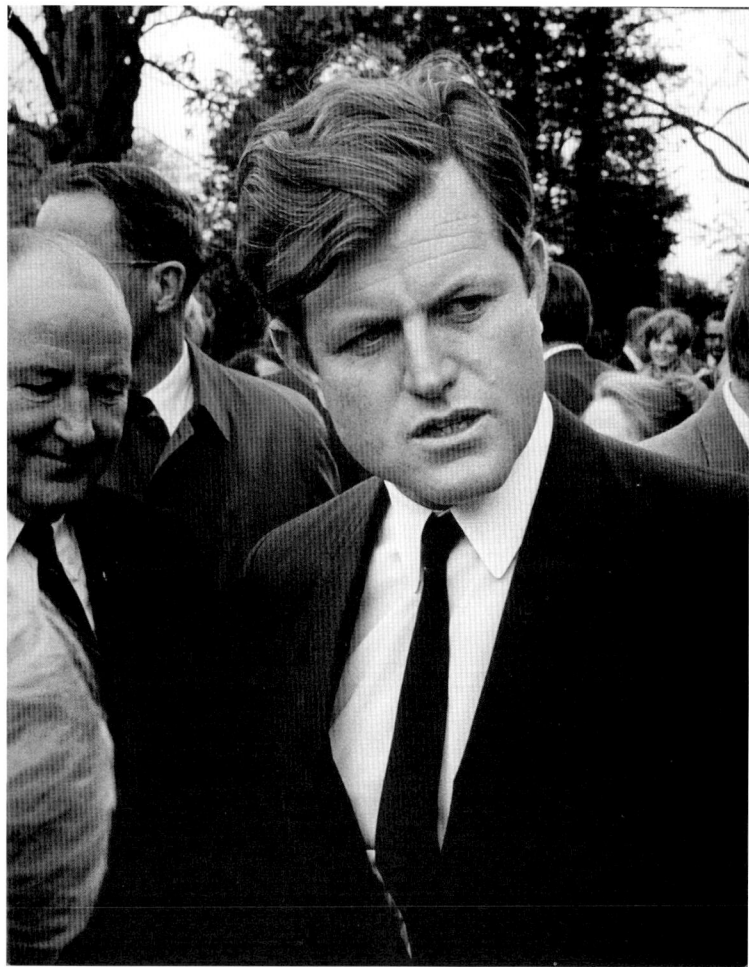

[Ted Kennedy confronts
reporters after incident
at Chappaquiddick.]
1968

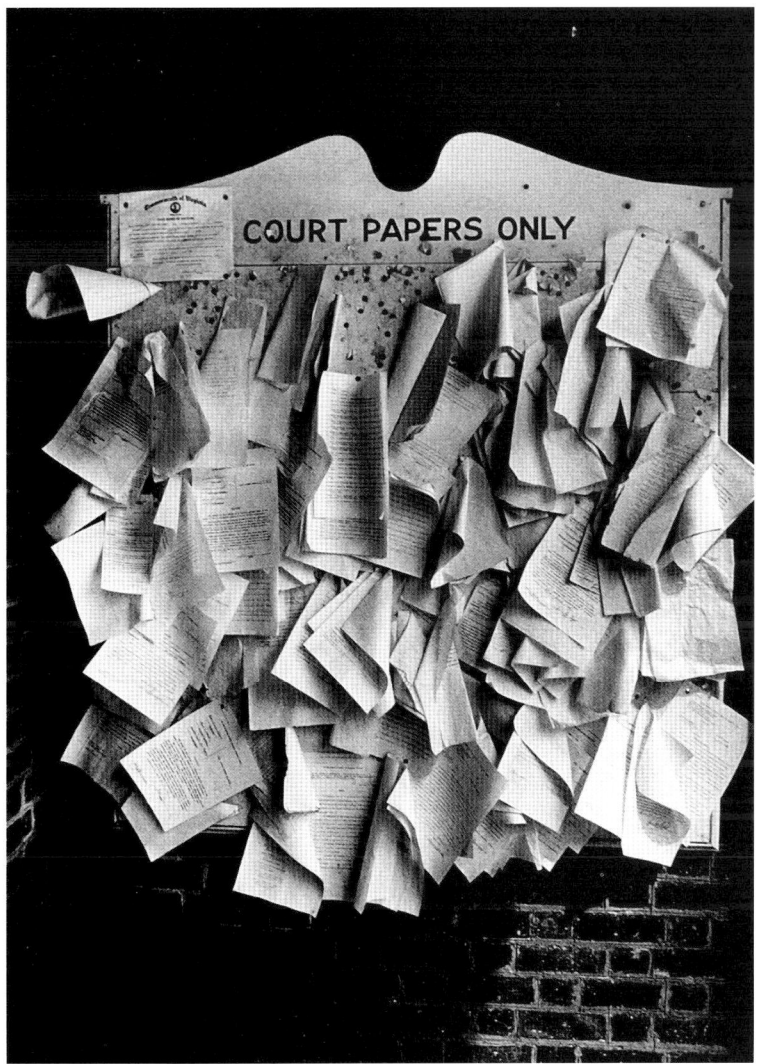

[Court Papers Only,
Fairfax County, VA.]
1976

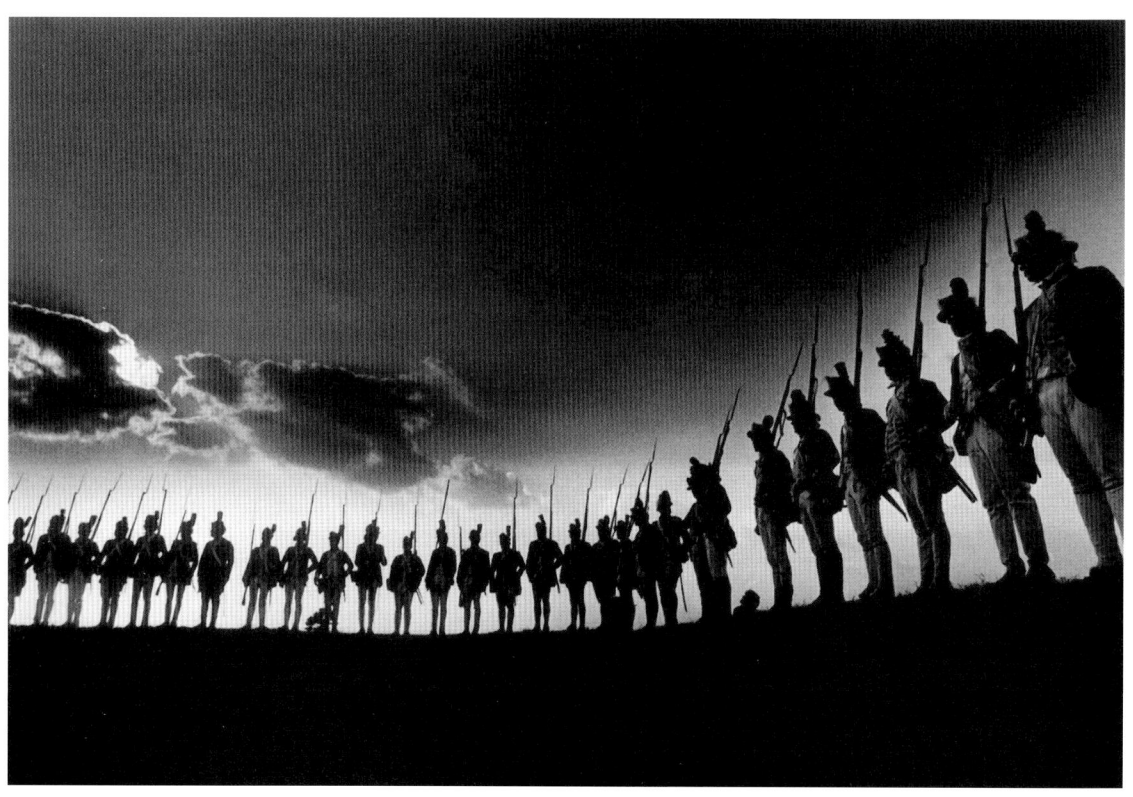

[Re-enactment of the 1781
Battle of Yorktown.]
1975
Digital print

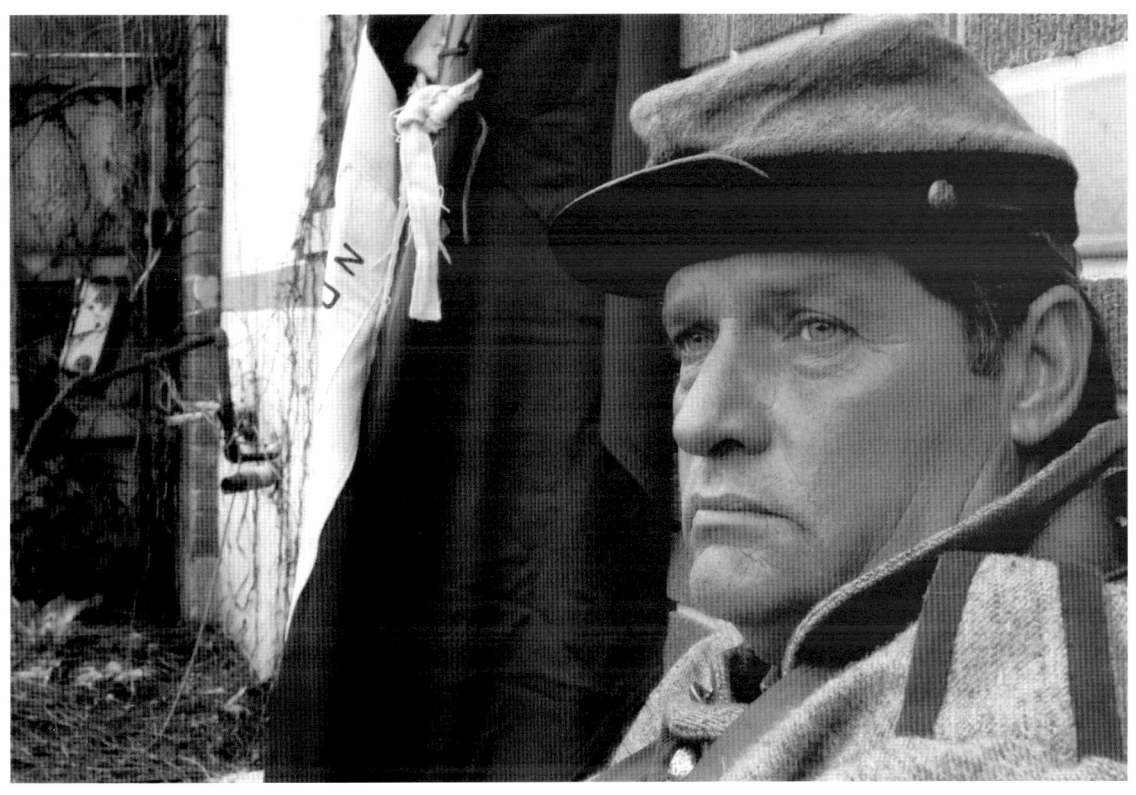

[Civil War reenactor]
1975
Digital print

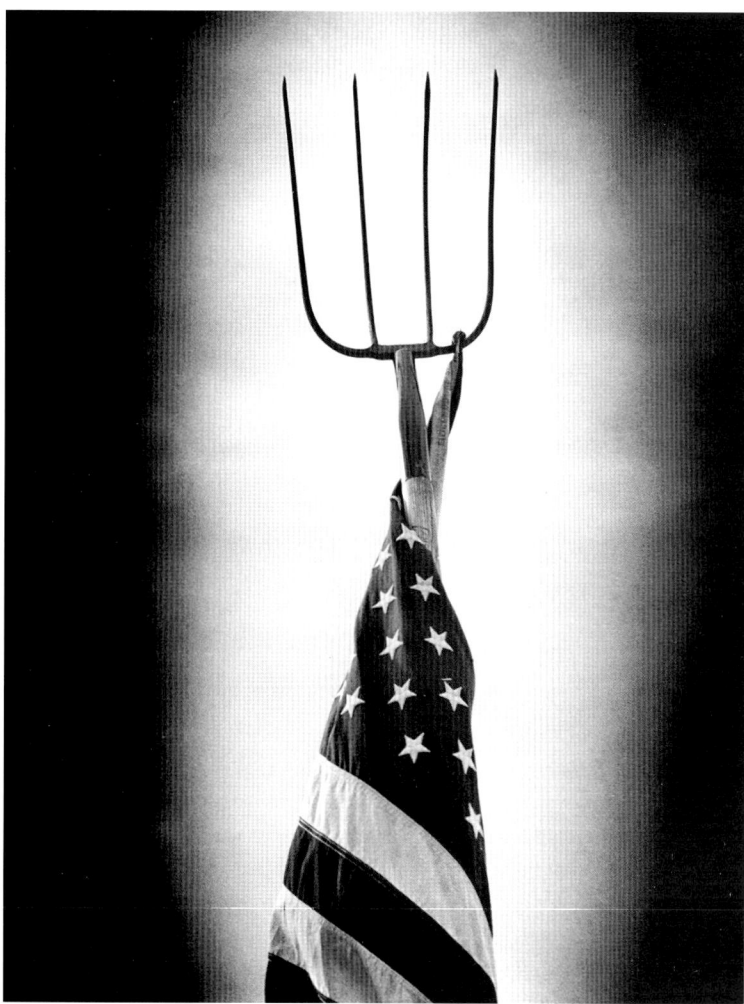

Farmers come to
Washington to protest.
Their symbol was a hayfork
and American flag.
1978

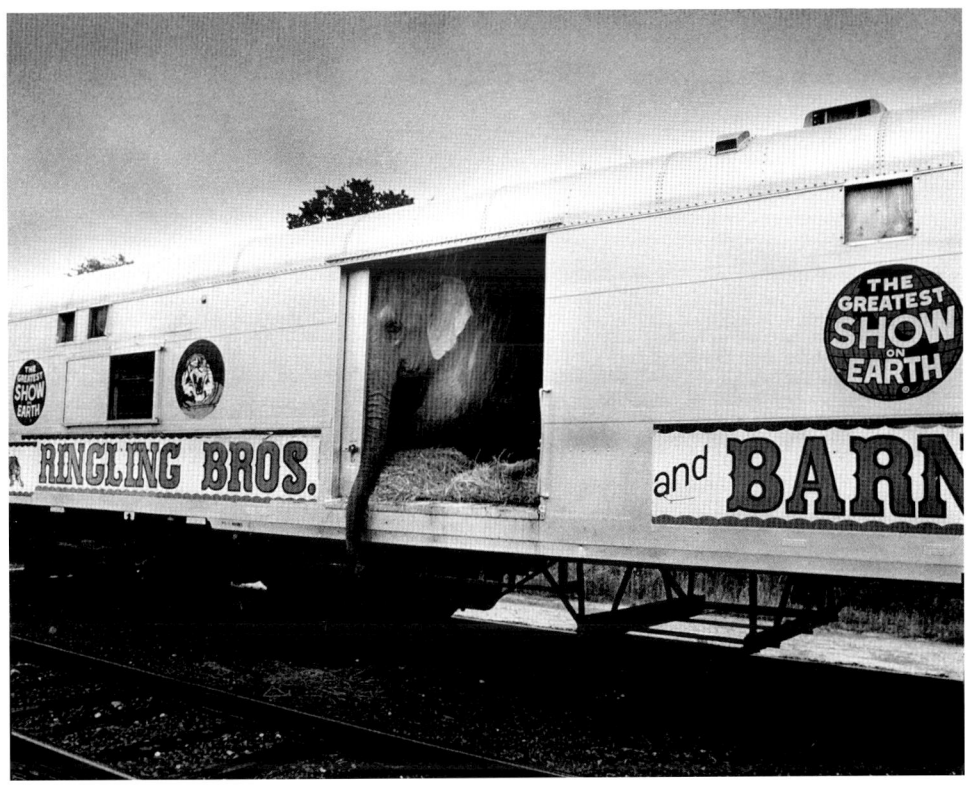

Peek-A-Boo Elephant,
16 May 1978
[An elephant looks out the
door of its car on the Ringling
Brothers Circus Train.]
1978

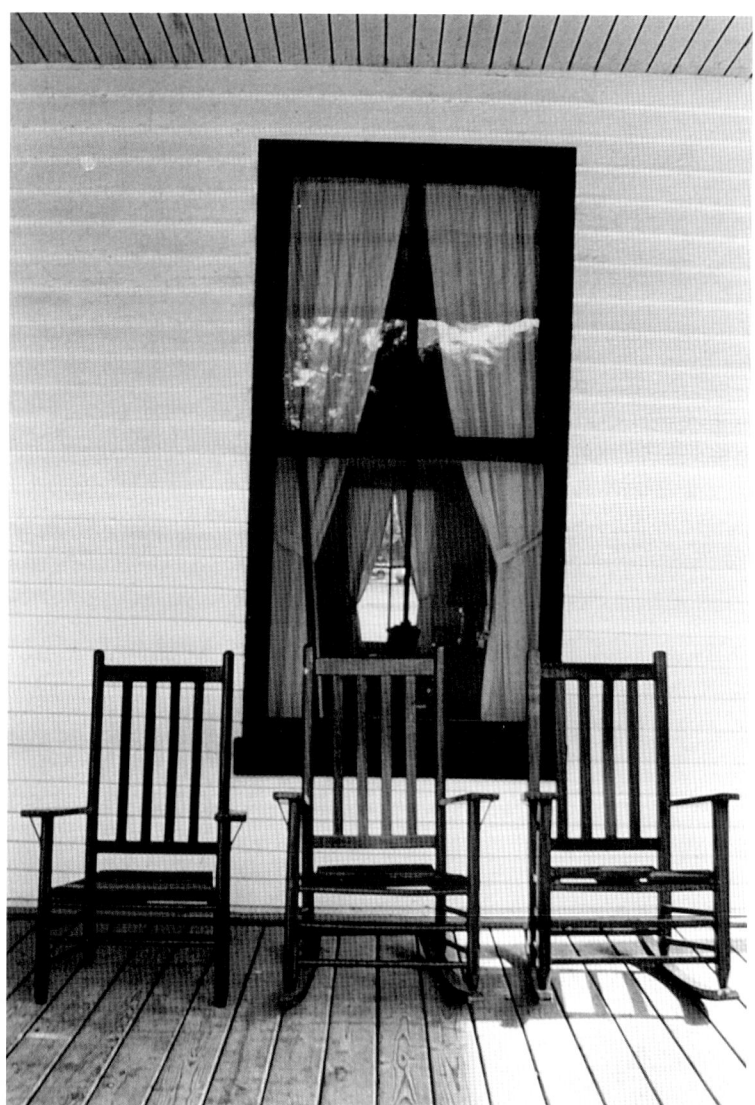

[Three chairs on a porch
in front of window.]
ca. 1978

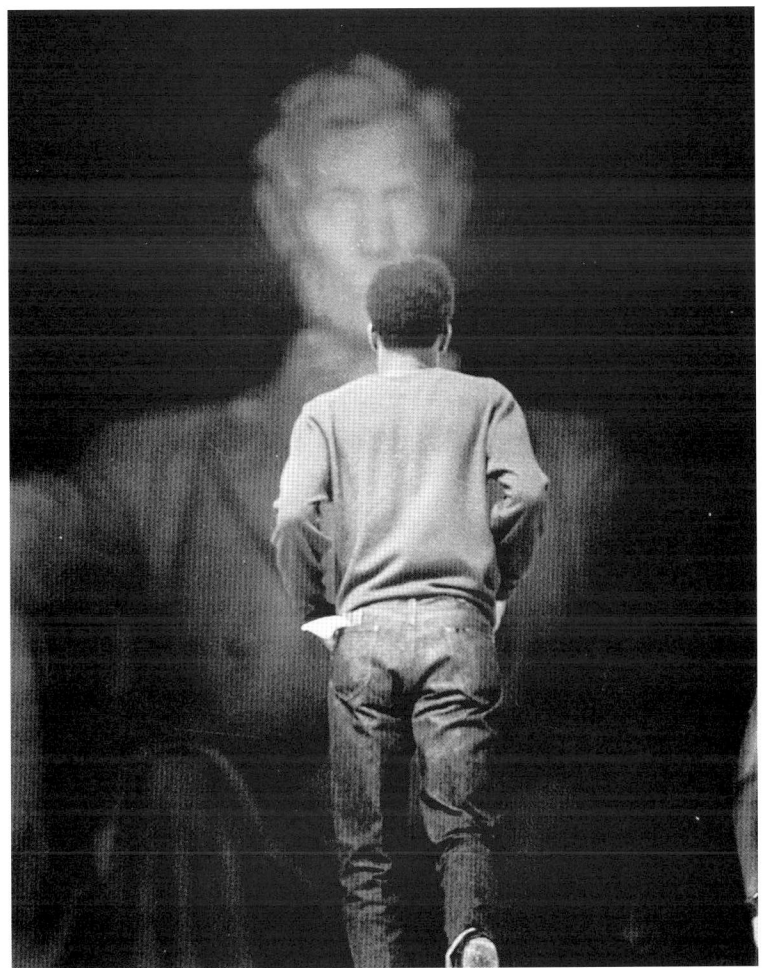

[Back of young man in blue jeans in front of Lincoln Memorial.]
1978

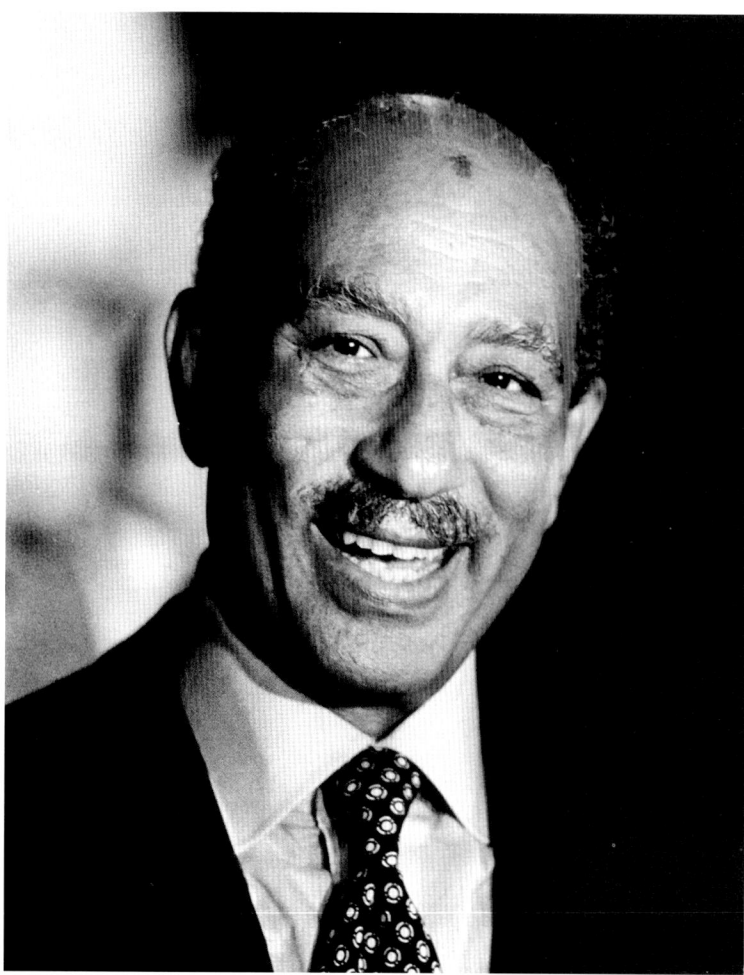

Anwar Sadat
[President of Egypt]
1978

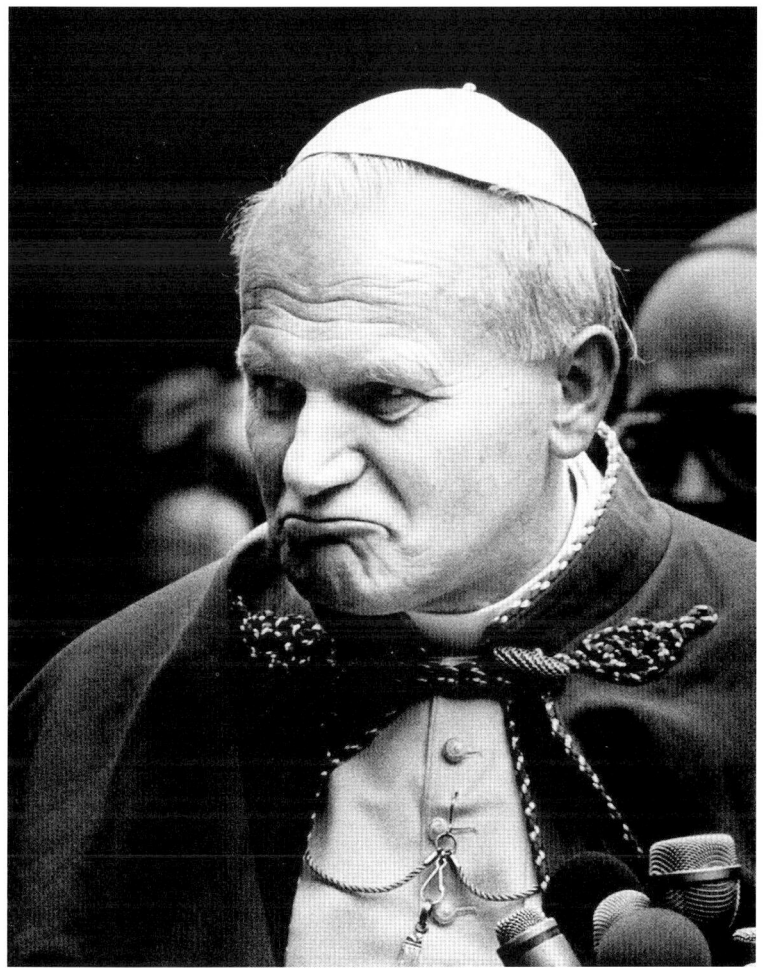

Pope John Paul II gives a stern
look as he answers questions
from the press, 6 October 1979.
1979

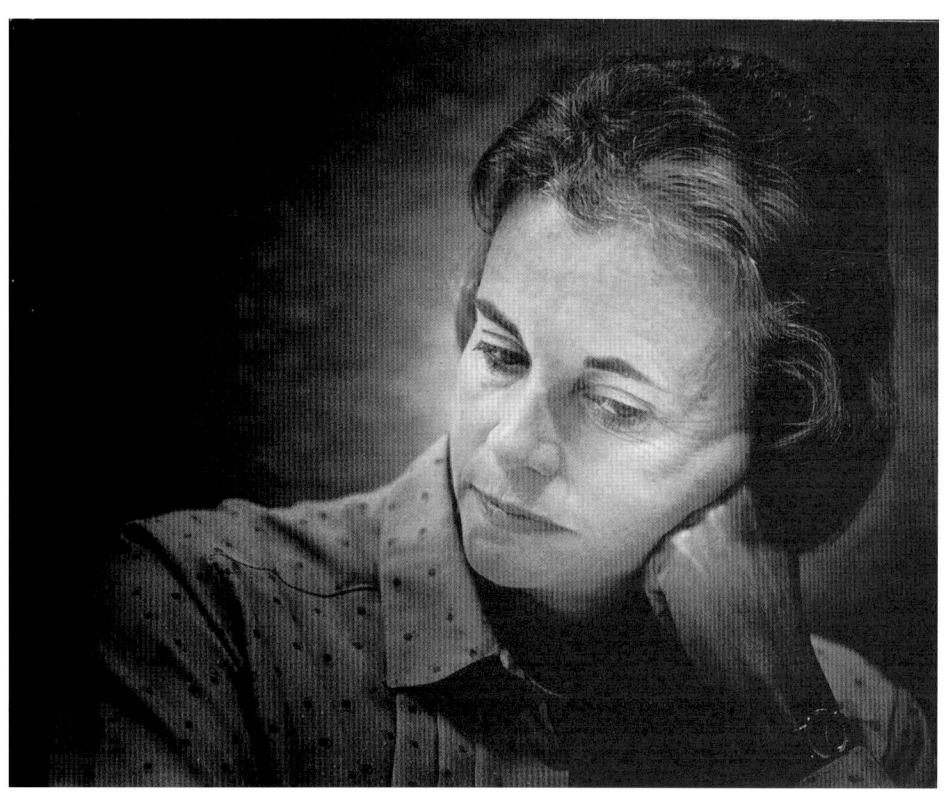

Ms. Justice
[Portrait of Sandra Day O'Connor]
1981

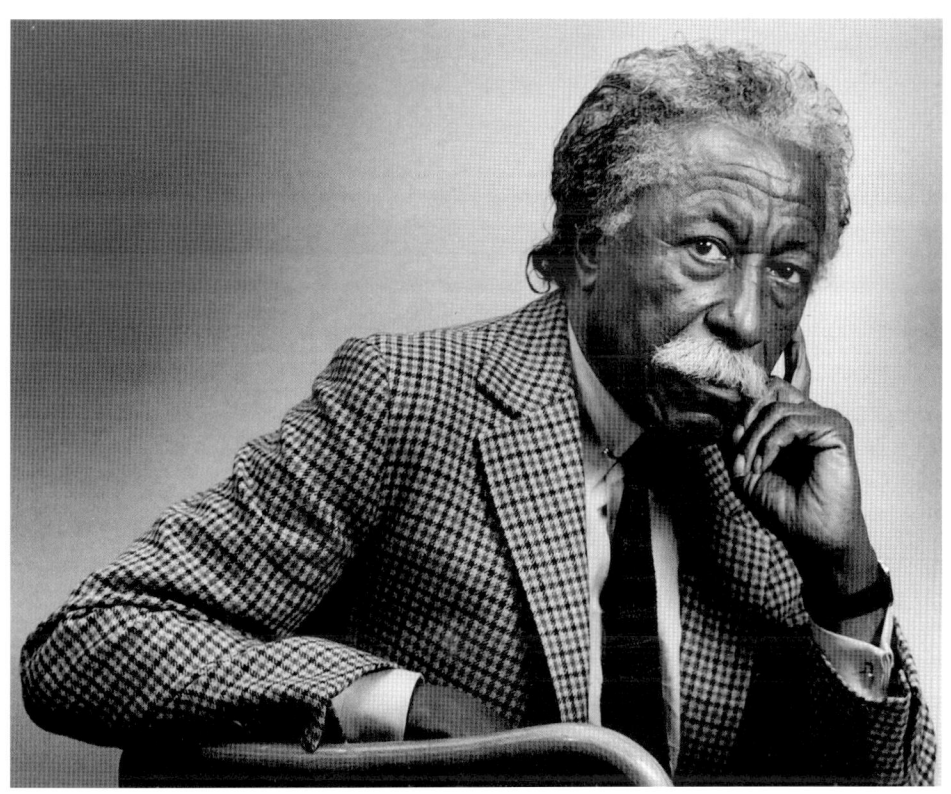

[Gordon Parks]
ca. 1980

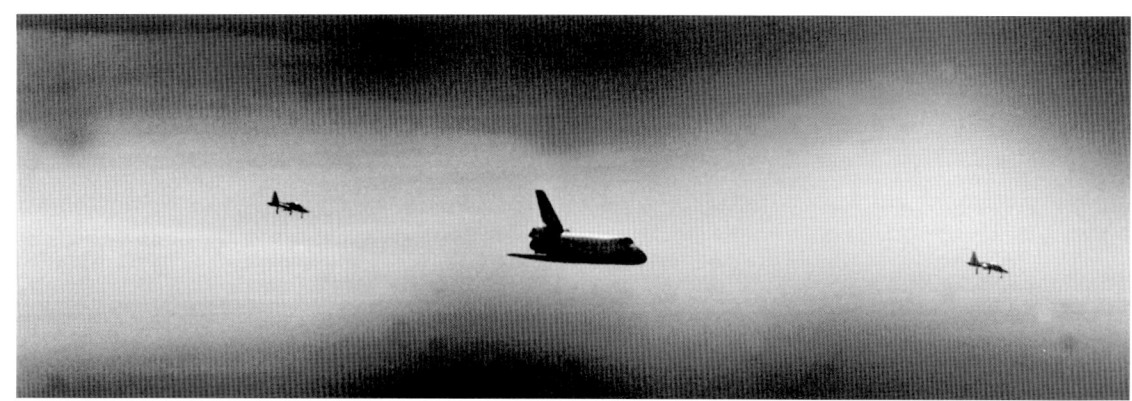

[The space shuttle Columbia
returns home from its first
mission in space.]
1981
Digital print

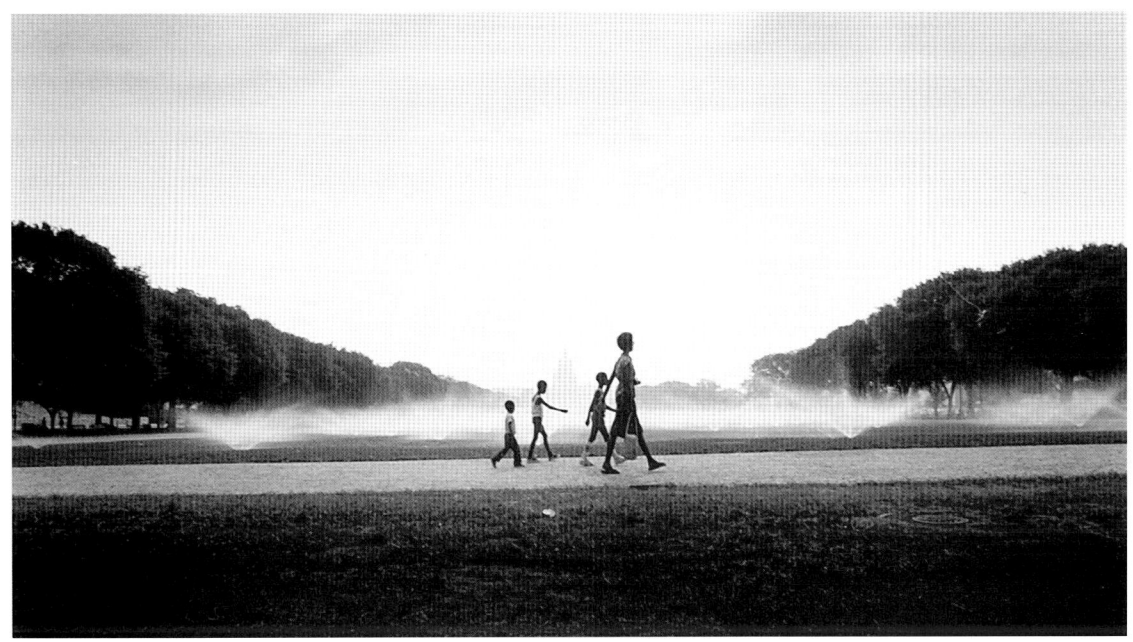

[Woman and children walk across
the Mall in Washington, DC with the
Capitol Building in the background.]
ca. 1980

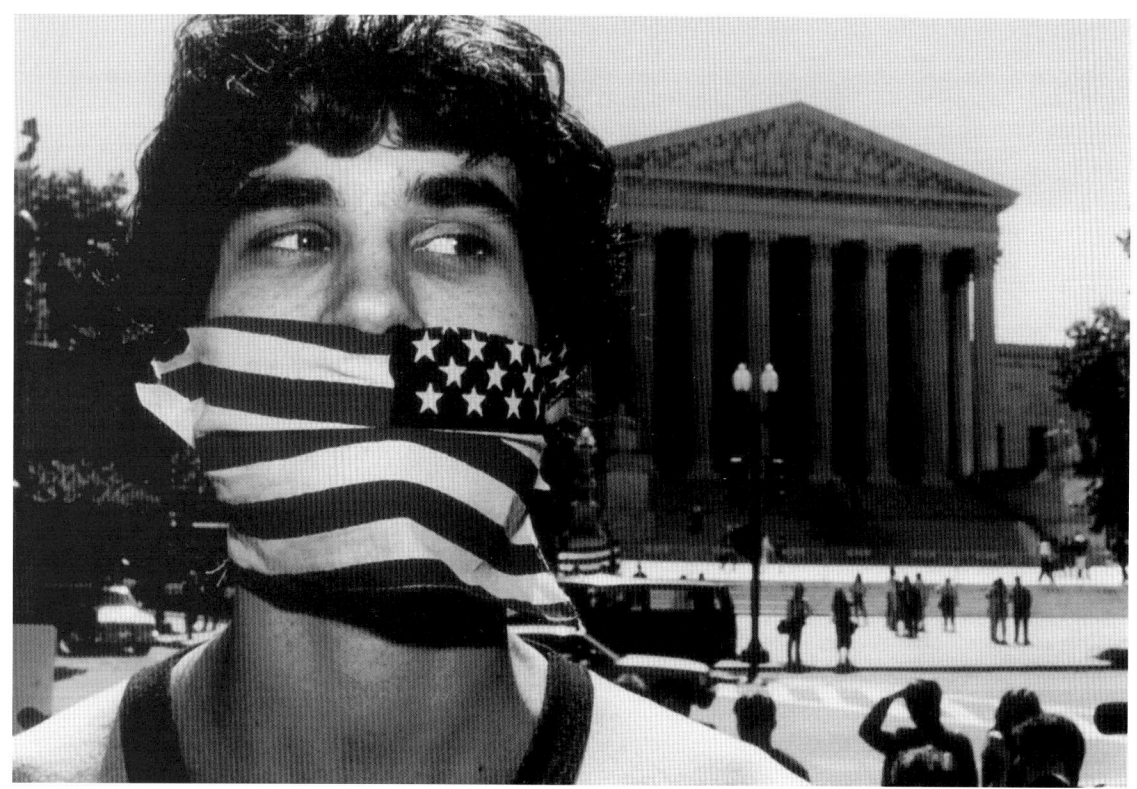

[Young man with his mouth
wrapped in the American flag in
front of the Supreme Court during
its deliberation of the legality of
burning the American flag.]
ca. 1980
Digital print

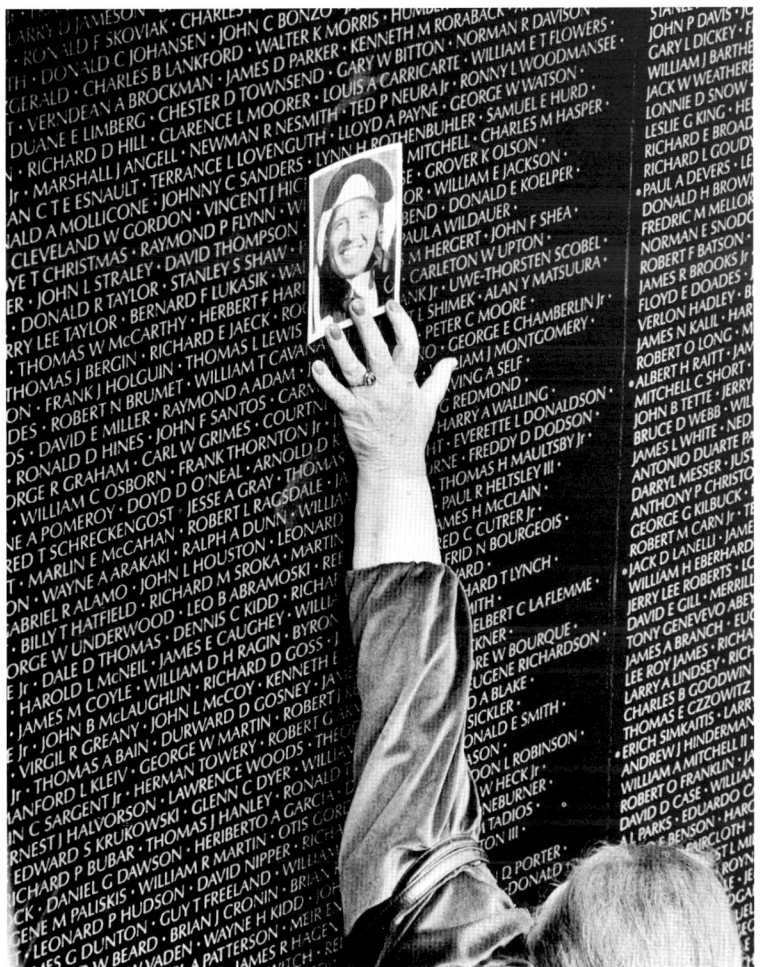

Vietnam Remembered
Vietnam Mother, Mrs. Ted Neura
holds picture of son who was
killed in Vietnam—near his
name at memorial,
11 November 1982.
1982

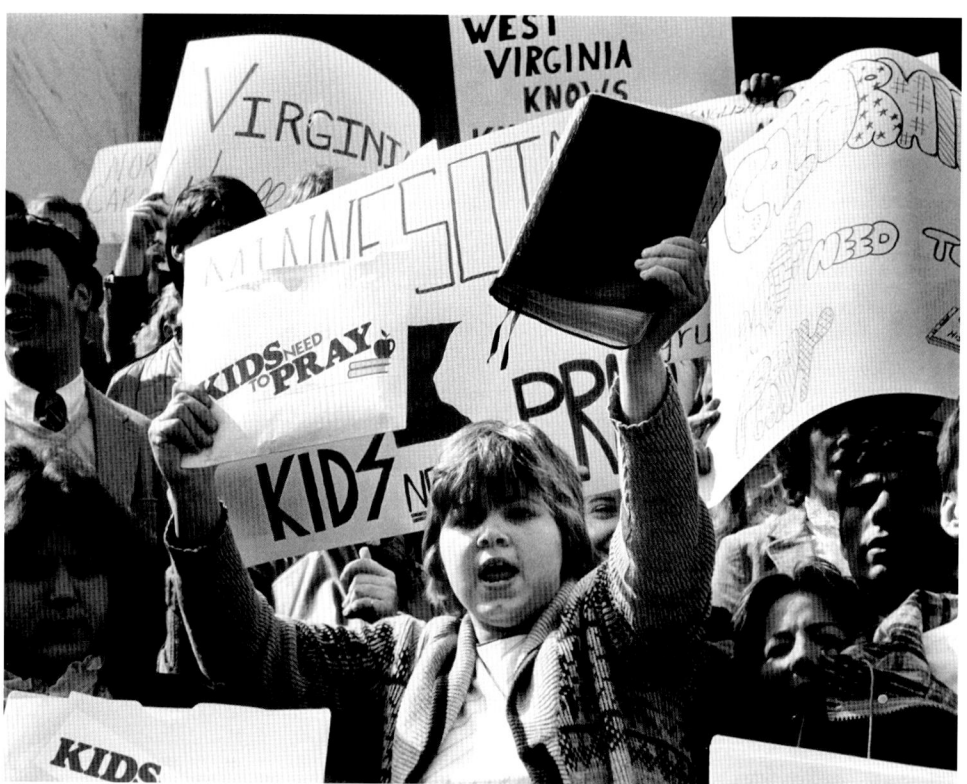

Kids need to pray
Kids demonstrate for school prayer
on Capital [sic] steps, 7 March 1984.
1984

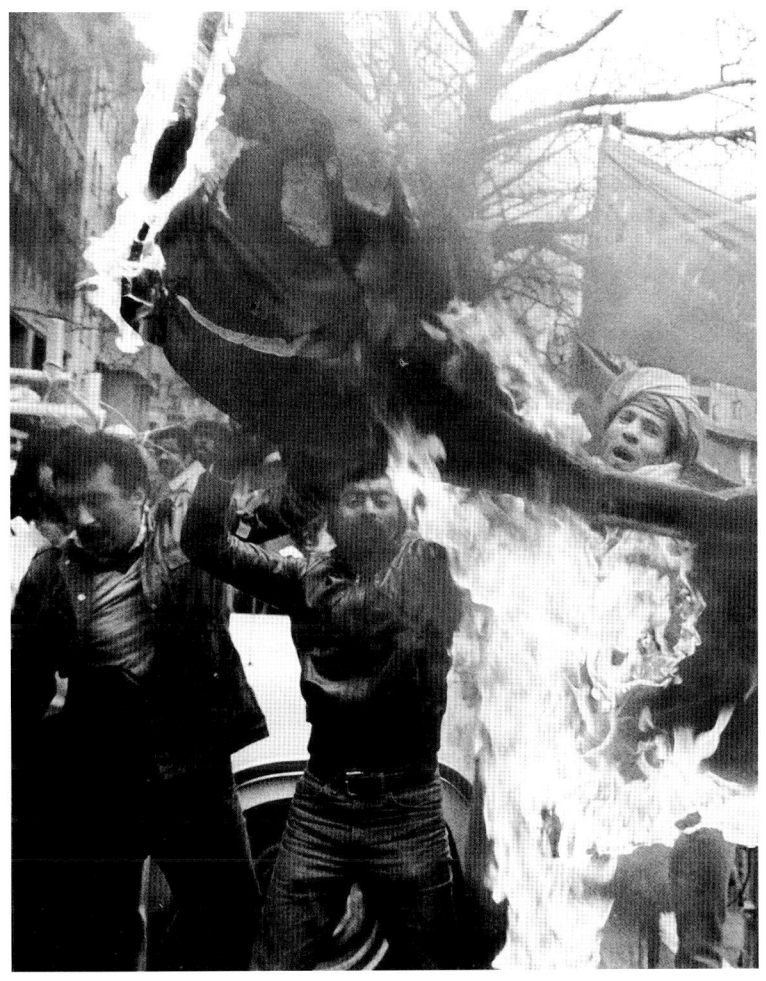

Protest
Afghanistan protestors burn
Soviet flag at Russian Embassy.
1982
Los Angeles Times Photo
by Bernie Boston

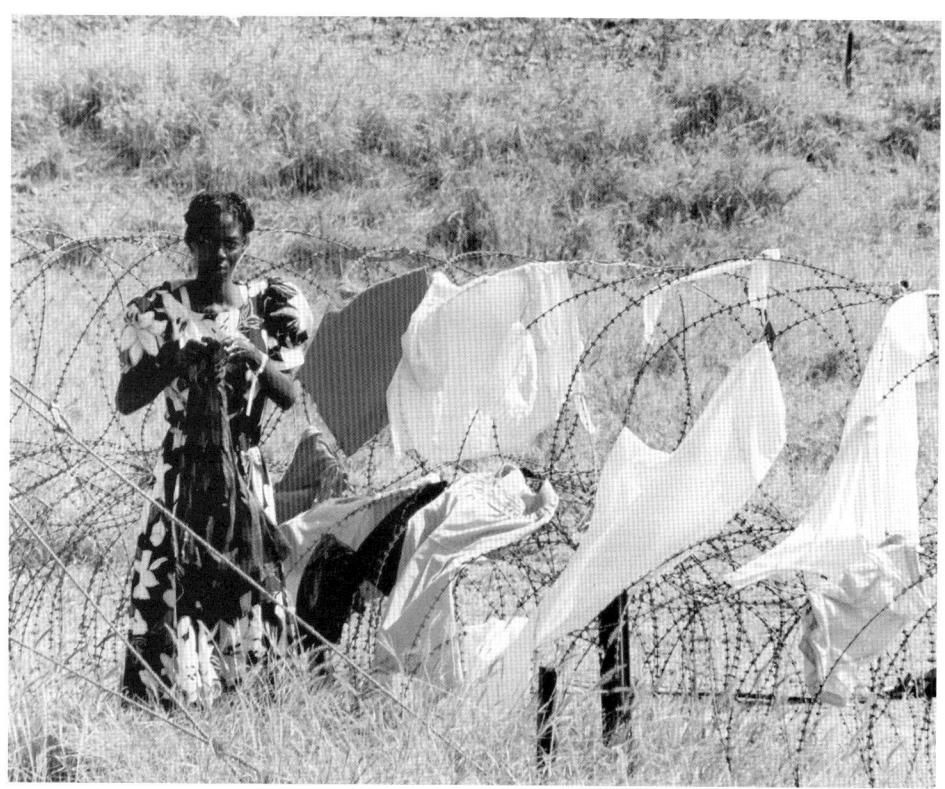

Wash Day
A Haitian woman hangs wash
on barbed wire in compound at
Gautanamo [sic] Naval Base,
22 November 1991.
1991
Los Angeles Times Photo
by Bernie Boston

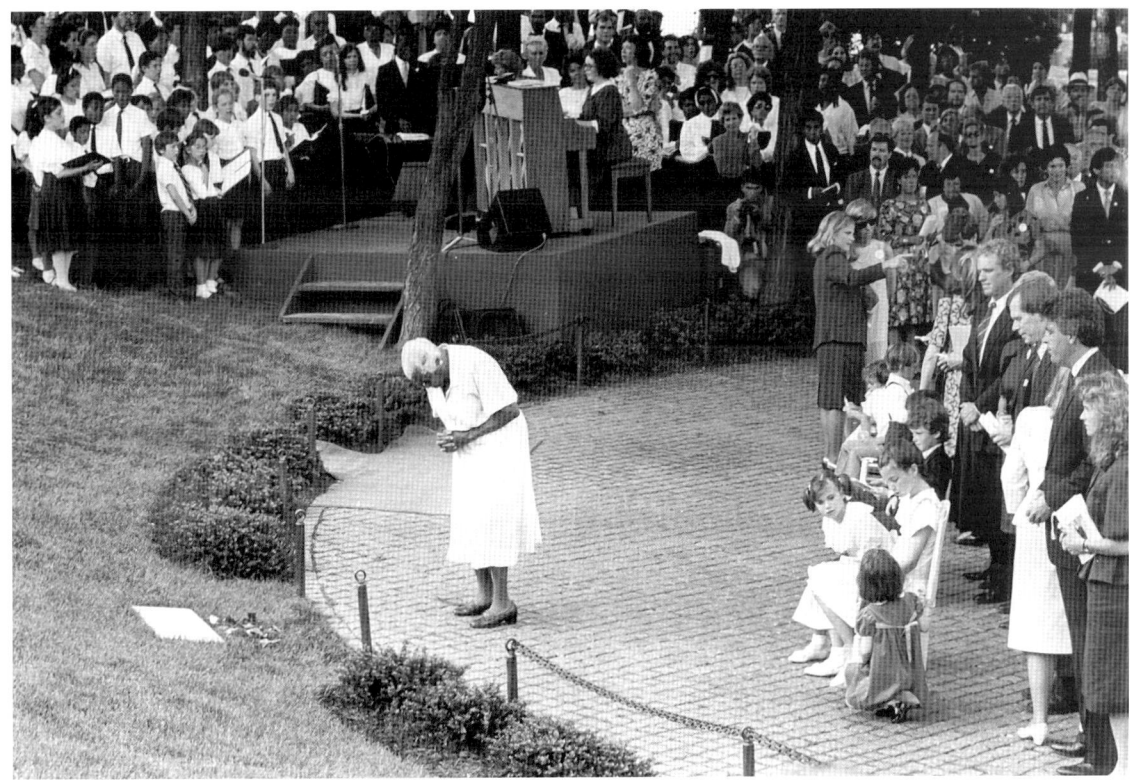

Washington DC, 6 June 88. Arlington
Cemetery. The nanny for the Kennedy
family pays respect at the graveside of
Robert F. Kennedy during memorial
services. The Kennedy family stands
in the back.
1988
News wire photograph
Los Angeles Times Photo
by Bernie Boston

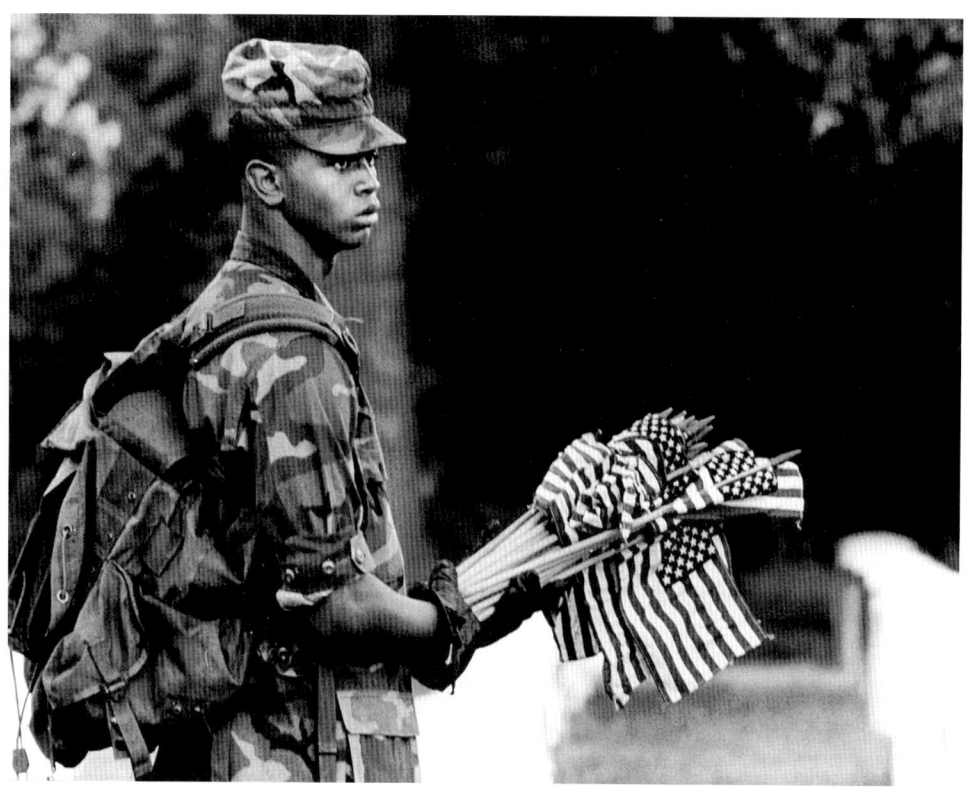

Tribute to comrads [sic]
Soldier places flags at gravestones
in Arlington National Cemetery for
Memorial Day.
1988
Los Angeles Times Photo
by Bernie Boston

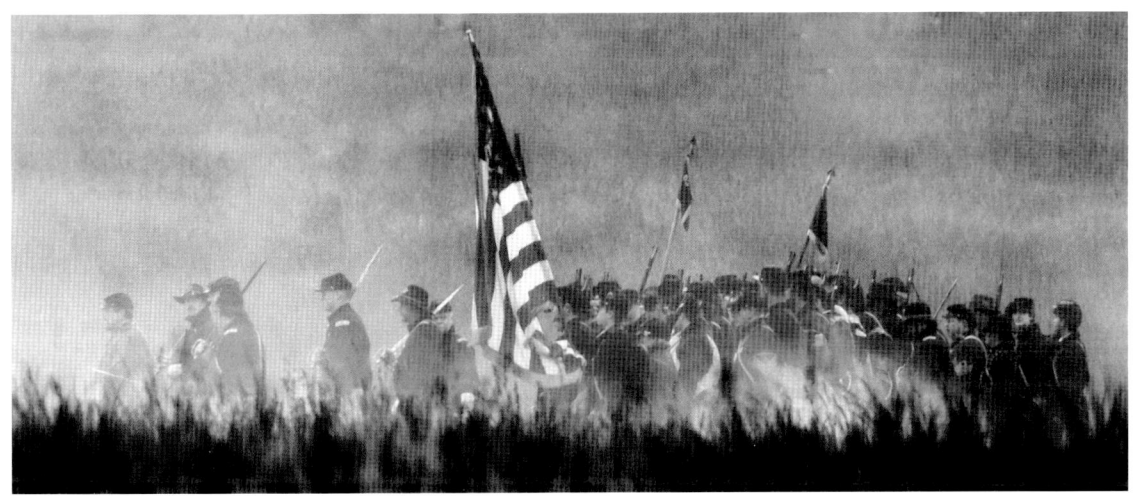

[Civil War re-enactment]
Marching through the "Field
of Lost Shoes" from the Battle
of New Market in Shenandoah
County, VA.
2004
Digital print

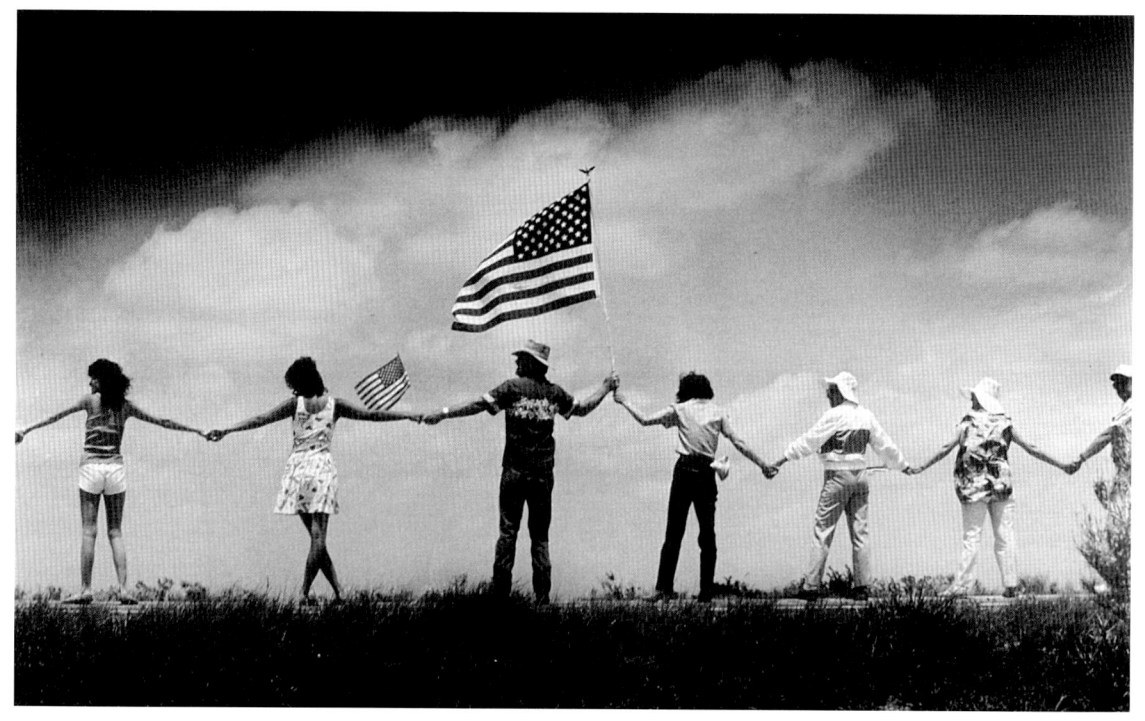

[A view of participants in *Hands Across America* event on May 25, 1986.]
1986

CHRONOLOGY

1933 Born on May 18 in Washington, DC, the only child of Dick and Norrine Boston, who passed on to him his all-American heritage of Native American, African and Irish ancestry. He spent his pre-school years in Washington, DC and then in Yellow Springs, OH, before returning to Washington.

1940 Moved with his parents to McLean, VA where he would live the majority of the next 54 years. However, he attended school in Washington, DC where the schools at that time were superior to those in then-rural Virginia.

1949 Photographed President Harry S. Truman in his Inaugural Parade. Since that time Boston photographed every seated U.S. president up through and including Bill Clinton.

1952 Graduated from Armstrong Technical High School, Washington, DC, where he was an ROTC cadet and scholastic sports photographer for the *Washington Daily News* newspaper.

1955 Graduated from the Rochester Institute of Technology (RIT), Rochester, NY, where he earned a degree in photo science. While at RIT he served as president of the student body, was a member of the fencing team and Sigma Pi fraternity, and was a founding member of the Delta Lambda Epsilon professional photo fraternity. In his last two years at RIT he was a member of the Washington, DC Air National Guard. After graduation, he married and was drafted into the Army. He served for two years in Germany as an army medic in radiology.

1957 After his discharge from the Army, he returned to McLean, VA and worked in the Washington area as assistant manager for a custom color service, a commercial studio, and was a freelance photographer.

1963   Hired by the *Dayton Daily News*, Dayton, OH, his first job as a newspaper photojournalist. He was divorced while working in Ohio. Received numerous awards from the Ohio Press Photographers' Association while in Dayton.

1967   Recruited by the Washington *Evening Star*, Washington, DC as a photojournalist, and moved back to McLean, VA.

In October he took a picture at an anti-Vietnam War march on the Pentagon that would become his trademark photograph, entitled *Flower Power*. The picture highlights a semi-circle of soldiers with rifles held out in front of them and a young man placing carnations in the soldiers' rifle barrels.

1968   *Flower Power* awarded second place for the Pulitzer Prize in news photography. It also received first place in the annual competitions of the National Press Photographers Association (NPPA), the White House News Photographers' Association (WHNPA), and the Washington-Baltimore Newspaper Guild, as well as numerous other contests. Boston was a consistent first-place winner in the NPPA, WHNPA and Guild competitions throughout his career at the *Star*.

1968–2006   Served on the faculty of many seminars, including the NPPA's Flying Short Course and the Southern Short Course; taught a photojournalism class at RIT in the spring of 1990 and a summer course in color photojournalism for seven summers; taught photojournalism at Northern Virginia Community College for several years; and continues to teach and mentor private students. He has judged national, state and local photo contests including the Leica Medal of Excellence, has been the subject of four television news features, and was featured in Nikon's "Masters of Photojournalism" video.

Flower Power continues to be published in hundreds of publications, including *The Best of LIFE*; *100 Photographs That Changed the World*; *LIFE: The First Fifty Years*; *150 Years of Photojournalism*; and a *LIFE* magazine special edition, *Classic Moments*. The photograph was selected by "Stars and Stripes" as one of the best 100 military images. It has also been published in many textbooks and appeared in the PBS series *American Photography: A Century of Images*.

Boston served four terms as president of the White House News Photographers Association (WHNPA), eight terms as vice president, and was on the executive board from 1973 to 1995. He served as chairman of NPPA's Freedom of Information Committee, and as president of its Washington chapter (now inactive).

1970	Married Peggy Peasley.
1971	Named director of photography at the *Star*, a position he held until the newspaper closed its doors in 1981.
	Received his private pilot's license and commercial license the following year.
1975	Named Outstanding Alumni at Rochester Institute of Technology (RIT).
1981	Recruited by the *Los Angeles Times* as its first Washington, DC bureau photographer, and set up and managed his own office and lab.
1991	Received the Kodak/WHNPA Achievement Award for service to his profession and the industry.
1993	Received the NPPA's Joseph A. Sprague Memorial Award, the organization's highest honor in the field of photojournalism.
1993	Retired from the *Los Angeles Times* on December 31.
1994	Moved to Basye, VA, in the Shenandoah Valley, where he became involved in local organizations such as the Shenandoah Valley Music Festival, the Lions Club and other service organizations.
1996	Inducted into the Hall of Fame of Sigma Delta Chi, the Society of Professional Journalists.
2000	Received his college fraternity's National Founders Award, its highest honor for an alumnus.
	Along with his wife, Peggy, he purchased the *Bryce Mountain Courier*, a monthly feature-oriented newspaper circulated throughout the Shenandoah Valley. He serves as publisher and continues his work as a photojournalist.
2001	Received the Distinguished Alumnus Award from RIT's College of Imaging Arts and Sciences.
2003	Purchased a local radio station as part of an LLC, where he worked as general manager until the station was sold in 2006.

2005   Received a first place award from the Virginia Press Association's annual contest for a photograph in the *Bryce Mountain Courier*.

2006   Received a first and a second place award from the Virginia Photographers' Association for *Courier* photographs.

            In October, a retrospective exhibition of his life's work is held in the School of Photographic Arts and Sciences Gallery at RIT.

Chronology compiled by Peggy Boston

COLOPHON

Designed by Marnie Soom / RIT Cary Graphic Arts Press

Typeset in Scala designed by Martin Majoor

Printed on 100 lb Matrix gloss text, .10 pt Carolina c1s cover

Printed by Rochester Offset Press

Supported by Nikon Professional Services

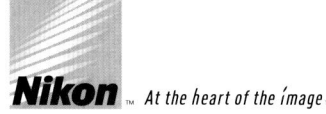 At the heart of the image ™